Victorian
DREAM HOMES

Home Planners, Inc.

Designed and Produced by Home Planners
Book Designer: Kathleen A. Koopman

Published by Home Planners
Editorial and Corporate Offices:
3275 West Ina Road, Suite 110
Tucson, Arizona 85741

Distribution Center:
29333 Lorie Lane
Wixom, Michigan 48393

Rickard D. Bailey, President and Publisher
Cindy Coatsworth Lewis, Publications Manager
Paulette Mulvin, Senior Editor

Photo Credits
Front Cover: Greg Ryan/Sally Beyer
Back Cover: Andrew D. Lautman

10 9 8 7

Library of Congress Catalog Card Number: 91-072540
ISBN: 0-918894-90-5 paperback
ISBN: 0-918894-91-3 hardback

On the front cover: Our charming Queen Anne front cover design is plan M3382. For more information about this home, see page 74.
On the back cover: This inviting Queen Anne design is our plan M9055. For more information about this home, see page 18.

TABLE OF CONTENTS

THE VICTORIAN ROMANCE 4

LARRY W. GARNETT AND ASSOCIATES, INC.
Profile 9
Victorian Plans 10
Farmhouse Plans 48
Blueprint Information 64

HOME PLANNERS
Profile 65
Victorian Plans 66
Farmhouse Plans 100
Blueprint Information 122

HISTORICAL REPLICATIONS, INC.
Profile 123
Victorian Plans 124
Farmhouse Plans 166
Blueprint Information 178

Great Outdoor Projects 179
Price Index 186
Order Form 187
Additional Products 188
Additional Plan Books 190
Useful Finishing Sources 192

EDITOR'S NOTE

Within these pages are the finest Victorian and Victorian-inspired Farmhouse designs available on the market today. Three master architectural design firms—Larry W. Garnett & Associates, Inc.; Home Planners, A Division of Hanley-Wood, Inc.; and Historical Replications, Inc.—are each showcased in separate sections featuring first the designer's special portfolio of Victorian homes followed by a delightful collection of Farmhouse plans. Experts in traditional home design, these designers interpret both cherished styles in distinctive ways, maintaining historical integrity while adding modern livability. And because complete blueprint packages are available for every spectacular home presented, the Victorian and Farmhouse plans you see here can be extended beyond mere admiration to actual construction and day-to-day enjoyment. If you've been searching for a home that is a reflection of this era of architecture, this book is the answer to your quest.

THE VICTORIAN ROMANCE

ew periods of architecture have received as much attention and spawned as many devotees as the 70 years from 1840 to 1910 known as the Victorian Era. Named after Queen Victoria, who enjoyed an uncommonly long reign (1837–1901), this period captures the imagination of so many people because so much seemed to change and blossom over its duration. Even though the architecture of the time had its antecedents in the Gothic Revival that began a few years earlier, it is the Victorian Era that most people embrace because it epitomizes what had been lacking or stale in architecture for hundreds of years: liveliness, whimsy and, above all, freedom of expression.

Like most movements that develop and evolve over a broad expanse of time, no single individual or event seemed to drive the Victorian Revolution. Rather, a series of stirrings, ideas and concepts— aided by technology—pushed the movement from one stage to another until it reached a grand climax near the end of the century.

REACTION TO CLASSICISM

First came a general uneasiness and backlash against the classicism of the early 19th Century. Greek Revival, characterized by formality, symmetry and "high-style," was perfectly suited to a new Republic that was enjoying the fruits of democracy and its newly won independence. However, after some 40 years of architecture marked by equal-spaced columns, carved entablature and severe granite facades, some people began to look for a fresh pattern for public and private residences. Andrew Jackson Downing supplied this when he published his *Victorian Cottage Residences* in 1842. The first popular pattern book for house styles, this publication supplied an alternative to the "perfect" Greek house facade—new fashions that took their cue from Medieval precedents and the Italian Renaissance.

Still anchored to antiquity and thus acceptable, this new style began to soften the edges of buildings, offering curved lines, arched windows, fretwork and even spires. Soon neighborhoods began to sport an "Italianate" cottage or "Medieval" manse worked in between imposing Greek residences. Suddenly, people had a choice and it was permissible to experiment with and broaden architectural expression, even going so far as to include exotic Egyptian or Oriental-inspired dwellings. Like a breath of fresh air, the winds of the Gothic Revival swept throughout England and America and the new architectural freedom was soon in full swing.

Classic Greek Revival

Medieval Architecture

HELP FROM TECHNOLOGY

Intellectual and artistic fervor alone would not have carried the movement far had not industrialization and technology been there to bear it up. The Industrial Revolution in both England and the United States supplied the material that fueled the fire of the New Freedom. The new wealth created by industrialization meant that an emerging middle and upper-middle class now had the resources to begin building homes of greater distinction and individualization. The "railroading" of America brought lumber, glass and metals in plentiful supply, while newly forged cutting and carving tools meant that craftsmen could give full vent to their woodworking acumen. Later in the century, the new "balloon-framing" technique freed builders from heavy, restrictive timber-framing methods and allowed houses to be built faster, more economically and, important to the movement, with many more asymmetrical wings, appendages and juttings.

No surprise that as Gothic Revival turned to full Victorian Romanticism, houses began to exhibit more and more handiwork in all areas. Builders during the High Victorian Era sought to outdo one another with more spindles, scallops, fretwork, brackets and carvings than the house before. Buildings sprouted domes and spires. Gables protruded in every direction. Floors overhung floors and were propped up by elaborately decorated columns. Perhaps the zenith of the movement came with the construction of the Carson Mansion in Eureka, California in 1886. Trying to please a local lumber baron, builders outdid themselves with a 5-story Queen Anne "castle" that sported multiple Gothic towers, exquisitely carved gables and friezes, finials on every conceivable roof cap, and a magnificent wraparound porch decorated with heavy balls and rings.

DEFINING THE PERIOD

Although it is romantically engaging to view the Victorian Era as an out-of-control architectural whirlwind sweeping toward the end of the century, the fact is that it was more prosaic than that. A number of architectural influences flourished at the time, but they were mostly derivative, and it is helpful in understanding the styles of the era to look at the various elements and how they interacted. For this discussion, I am indebted to Virginia and Lee McAlester, whose book, *A Field Guide to American Houses* (Alfred A. Knopf, 1984), does the best and quickest job of sorting out these styles and establishing their chronology.

Gothic Revival Architecture

ROMANTIC BEGINNINGS

As already noted, *Gothic Revival* (1840-1880) was a direct reaction to—or relief from— the strict rules of form and composition established by Early Classical Revival and particularly Greek Revival. Gothic Revival style made use of a steeply pitched roof with cross-gables and windows patterned in a distinctive Gothic or Medieval shape. Probably the most characteristic feature of this style is the decorative *vergeboard*, or gable trim piece, that was often cut in scallop, fleur-de-lis or other patterns with the newly perfected scroll saw. More popular for rural areas, the design was too oversized and excessive for smaller urban lots. Thus, while heralding a new departure from classical symmetry and restraint, the style never really caught on widely and was on the wane by 1880. Nevertheless, it did set the precedent for future experimentation and its "dare-to-

The Carson Mansion

Italianate Style

Second Empire Style

be-different" attitude got the Romantic Era under-way.

Italianate Style (1840-1885), which surfaced about the same time as Gothic Revival, began in England as part of the Picaresque movement and was even more opposed to formal classical ideals. It emphasized Italian villa-style architecture with low-pitched roofs, wide overhangs, and tall, narrow windows frequently elaborated with hooded crowns or "eyebrows." A common characteristic was a central tower or cupola rising above the other parts of the building, often sporting a curved mansard roof. Popularized by Andrew Jackson Downing in his pattern books, this style was admired by many richer clientele and was widely built in various forms until the financial panic of 1873 and the resulting economic collapse. Built mostly of masonry, these houses contributed more to the romantic freedom of the era than they did to the craftsmanship and techniques employed in later wood-sided Victorian houses.

MIDDLE VICTORIAN PERIOD

Second Empire Style (1855-1885) took a few cues from the Italianate houses that were in vogue a few years earlier, but added modern rooflines and cornices taken from the French fashions of the day. Named after the reign of Napoleon III (1852-1870), France's Second Empire exerted a tremendous influence on the architecture of the period by sponsoring exhibitions in Paris in 1855 and 1867. The most striking characteristic of this style is the dual-pitched, hipped mansard roof, named after 17th-Century French architect Francois Mansart whose work was revived at the time. These roof lines—commonly straight, straight with a flair, or slightly concave—graced all sides of the building,

as well as any cupolas or towers that ascended above the main structure. Dormer windows appeared in abundance on Second Empire homes, and many featured Italianate brackets at the cornices and decorative iron railings or crests at the highest roof line. Many public buildings or private residences were built or remodeled in this style in the mid-1800s, but like the Italianate, this European-influenced style disappeared quickly following the financial panic of 1873 and the economic hard times that followed.

Stick Style (1860-1890) refocused builders on the use of wood instead of masonry as was often used in European styles. However, unlike their romantic Gothic forebears which made use of fancy

Stick Style

fretwork and detailing at doors, windows and cornices, Stick houses used the plane of the wall as a decorative element. Structures were quite simple and box-like, but the faces of walls were "tricked up" with patterns of horizontal, vertical or diagonal boards raised from the wall surface for emphasis. In addition, exposed and embellished trusses were shown under the peaks

Queen Anne Style

of gables and beneath overhanging eaves. Called "stickwork," this construction technique carried the romantic notion of "honesty of style" since it showed the structural nature of the building. However, unlike earlier half-timbering which was integral to the framing of the building, stickwork was simply applied over light balloon framing and had nothing to do with supporting the structure. Nonetheless, proponents argued the value of the look with its return to natural materials and the style was very popular well into the 1880s in areas with an abundance of lumber.

HIGH VICTORIAN PERIOD

Queen Anne Style (1880-1910) was the culmination of the romantic quest for fine craftsmanship, abundance of detail and free individual expression. Popularized by a group of 19th-Century architects led by Richard Norman Shaw, the name was actually misapplied and inappropriate, since Queen Anne's reign (1702-1714) produced more formal and heavy Renaissance-Style architecture. Nevertheless, the romantic notion of this Medieval period was more important than actuality, and the name quickly caught on and stuck. At first characterized by heavier half-timbering in England, the Queen Anne Style rapidly evolved in this country to more elaborate and delicate structures featuring patterned shingles, carved fretwork, finials and lacelike wooden ornamentation throughout the building.

Two of the most common sub-types of the Queen Anne Style are defined by their particular type of decorative detailing. *Spindlework* types feature delicately turned porch supports and spindle-type ornamentation, particularly in porch balustrades or as a frieze hung from the porch ceiling. Often referred to as "gingerbread," spindlework ornamentation is commonly found in gable ends and under wall overhangs. *Free Classic* types use classical columns, rather than turned posts, as porch supports. These porch-support columns are often grouped together in units of two or three. Other characteristics are formal dentils at the cornice line, Palladian windows and small front gables or pediments.

Queen Anne Victorians dominated residential building from about 1880 until 1900 and persisted in many parts of the United States through the first decade of this century. The style disappeared most quickly from the Northeast and Eastern Seaboard, where it was replaced principally by Colonial Revival fervor. However, excellent examples of Queen Anne Style continued to be built after this time in the San Francisco area, the Northwest and parts of the South.

Spindlework

Free Classic Columns

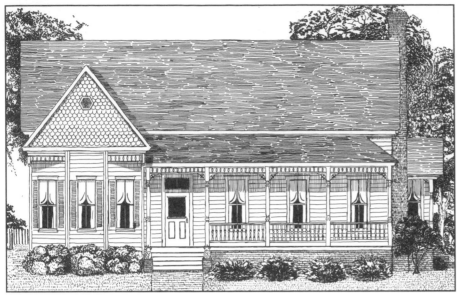

Folk Victorian

TURN-OF-THE-CENTURY ADAPTATIONS

The Romantic Movement was so pervasive that even as a new century dawned with divergent architectural prospects, Victorian influences still lingered and evolved in the twilight of its glory.

A fanciful new *Shingle Style* (1890-1910) enjoyed brief popularity at the turn of the century, especially in seaside resorts of the Northeastern United States. Rather than making use of fancy woodwork or detailing at doors, windows, cornices and other areas, the Shingle Style used a "cocoon" of shingles to envelop a complex architectural style. In fact, this skin of shingles often hid a number of interesting and dichotomous variations in forms and styles. However, still derivative, the Shingle Style borrowed the wide porches, asymmetrical forms and patterned shingles from the Queen Anne Style and the gambrel roofs and lean-to additions from the newly emerging Colonial Revival Style.

A by-product of the Victorian Era—lacelike porch detail and fancy brackets under the eaves—found its way into the simplest housing forms. After 1870, many basic folk houses began to sport Queen-Anne-Style porch supports, saw-cut cornice brackets and spindlework friezes suspended from porch ceilings. Although much less elaborate than their Victorian sisters, these houses became prevalent enough that a new style, *Folk Victorian* (1870–1910), was born. Local carpenters made good use of pre-cut Victorian trim pieces available at lumber yards and soon many people were enjoying front porches and gabled facades with a quaint Victorian look. After about 1910, these Folk Victorians—or Symmetrical Victorians as they are called by some scholars—generally lost favor as the country finally got its fill of fancy Victorian detailing and turned to other house styles for the new century.

GONE BUT NOT FORGOTTEN

The Victorian Era had a long, full flower of nearly 70 years. The emotional appeal of this family of fanciful, delicate, decorative architectural styles was so strong that it took the harsh realities of a World War and the nihilism of the 1920s to dispel it. Yet, the romance of this era never really died. Whenever society has too much of modern technology, warfare or rampant commercialism, it inevitably recycles itself back to an era that is quieter, softer and more romantic.

Grand Victorian Style is, after all, one of those rare pleasures that must be experienced more with the heart than with the intellect—to be viewed and appreciated without regard to cost, reason or rationale. Victorians exist simply to be admired and loved—one of the last, great romantic adventures in Architecture!

Rickard Bailey
Home Planners, Inc.

Shingle Style

LARRY W. GARNETT & ASSOCIATES, INC.

Larry W. Garnett & Associates, Inc. of Pasadena, Texas began designing homes for Houston-area residents in 1977. For the past ten years, Garnett & Associates has been marketing designs nationally to both individuals and builders, and the company's houses have now been built throughout the United States, and in Canada, Australia and Ireland.

A member of the American Institute of Building Design, Garnett & Associates has received numerous awards from the Texas Institute of Building Design, including several first-place awards for planned developments and builders' model homes. The firm recently received an award from the American Institute of Building Design for a custom home in Nashville.

In March 1985, the "Wall Street Journal Report," a syndicated television program, featured Garnett & Associates on a segment involving the increasing popularity of new Victorian homes and the availability of stock plans and designs for such homes. Recently, the company had the opportunity to design a twelve-home historic Hawaiian development in Kailua, Hawaii. This award-winning project features architecture that was popular in Hawaii in the early 1900s.

The company's plans have been published in such magazines as *House Beautiful, Country Living, Home,* and *Professional Builder.* Garnett's Victorian-inspired designs are featured each month in a regular column in *Victoria* magazine.

"American residential design during the last half of the 19th Century was dominated by the Victorian Style of architecture," relates Garnett. "Today, the homes from this period are considered by many to be symbols of the creative freedom and optimism that was prevalent during this period of rapid industrialization. While mass-produced tools and building materials were inexpensive and readily available, the homes were still constructed by artisans who took great pride in showcasing their craftsmanship. Furthermore, the designs for these homes were inspired by the classical architectural elements and forms that have withstood the test of time. Various details, such as gables, chimneys, steep rooflines and porches, provided traditional forms that were easily understood and emotionally comforting. The homes in this section utilize these same traditional values and provide a sense of continuity by linking the present to the past.

"Our Victorian and Farmhouse plans were designed to recapture the harmony of style and timeless design of this bygone era. Along with this nostalgic charm, we wanted to create homes that would become retreats from today's fast-paced society, with spacious living areas, multi-purpose media centers, and elegant master suites. The design knowledge we have accumulated from open-concept space planning, along with the realization that people also desire private, personal areas, has resulted in a blend of expansive areas with unobstructed views, along with versatile alcoves and cozy nooks for privacy.

"Based on original designs of the late 19th and early 20th Centuries, these homes range from the elaborate and ornate Queen Anne Style to the simple, decoratively detailed Folk Victorian Style. In addition, there are several examples of the Shingle Style, which were inspired by the fashionable summer resorts of the East Coast, with their massive, irregular rooflines, numerous windows and uniform shingle siding.

"As you browse through the following pages, we hope you agree that these designs offer a lasting tribute to the design integrity of the Victorian Era. Perhaps one of them will not only recall for you the comfort and serenity of the past, but also fulfill all the requirements you may have for your ideal home."

Classic exterior detailing transforms this otherwise simple design into an elegant Victorian cottage. The wraparound veranda is a perfect place for outdoor living. Inside, a raised foyer overlooks the large formal dining area and the living room. The kitchen offers a large built-in pantry, a bay-windowed breakfast nook and an island cooktop. Bedroom 2 features a fourteen-foot ceiling, bookcases and a plant ledge above the windows. Bedroom 3 has a delightful windowed alcove, perfect for a reading or study area. French doors open from the master bedroom to the veranda. The master bath features a corner tub and glass-enclosed shower, along with a dressing table and plenty of linen storage.

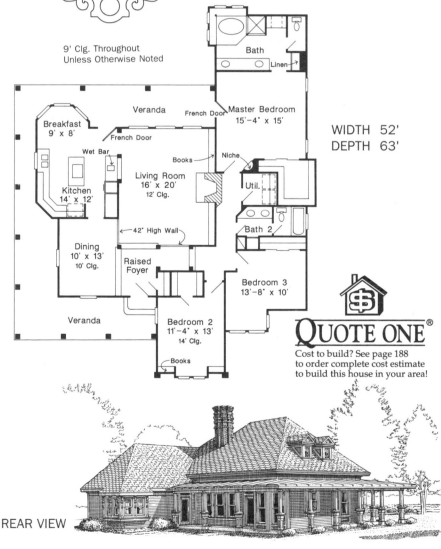

9' Clg. Throughout
Unless Otherwise Noted

Bath

Linen

Veranda

French Door

Master Bedroom
15'-4" x 15'

WIDTH 52'
DEPTH 63'

Breakfast
9' x 8'

French Door

Wet Bar

Books

Niche

Kitchen
14' x 12'

Living Room
16' x 20'
12' Clg.

Util.

42" High Wall

Bath 2

Dining
10' x 13'
10' Clg.

Raised
Foyer

Bedroom 3
13'-8" x 10'

QUOTE ONE®

Cost to build? See page 188 to order complete cost estimate to build this house in your area!

Veranda

Bedroom 2
11'-4" x 13'
14' Clg.

Books

DESIGN	M9049
BEDROOMS	3
BATHROOMS	2
SQUARE FOOTAGE	1,891
PRICE	A4

REAR VIEW

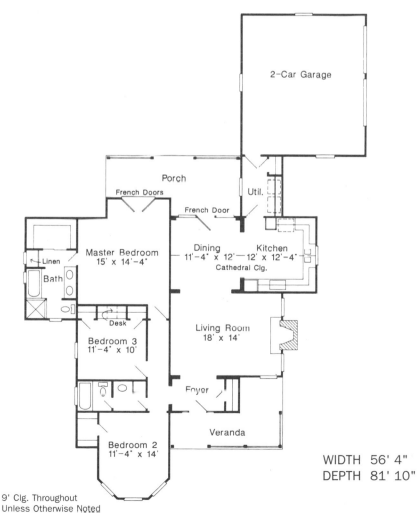

2-Car Garage

Porch

French Doors

French Door

Util.

Master Bedroom
15' x 14'-4"

Linen

Bath

Desk

Dining
11'-4" x 12'

Kitchen
12' x 12'-4"
Cathedral Clg.

Bedroom 3
11'-4" x 10'

Living Room
18' x 14'

Foyer

Veranda

Bedroom 2
11'-4" x 14'

9' Clg. Throughout
Unless Otherwise Noted

WIDTH 56' 4"
DEPTH 81' 10"

The ornate turned posts at the veranda, along with delicate wood molding and carved gable brackets, give this Queen Anne Style cottage lasting elegance. The dining area features triple French doors and a cathedral ceiling. Bedroom 3 offers a built-in desk, making it a perfect optional study. The master suite has French doors opening to a covered porch and a large bath with a walk-in closet, plenty of linen storage, and a glass-enclosed shower. The steep-pitched roof offers the opportunity to utilize the attic space for a 14' x 19' bonus room with a ½ bath. Plans are included for this option, showing a circular staircase located at the foyer closet area. An attached two-car garage is located conveniently just off the handy utility room.

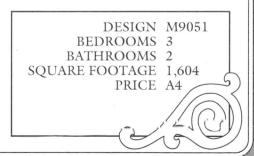

DESIGN M9051
BEDROOMS 3
BATHROOMS 2
SQUARE FOOTAGE 1,604
PRICE A4

The prominent octagon-shaped turret with leaded-glass transom windows is a Queen Anne Style detail typical of only the most elaborate one-story designs from the turn of the century. Inside, it creates a delightful space that can function as a conversation alcove or a study area. The kitchen has a center island and plenty of cabinet space. A ten-foot ceiling and three full-length windows in the dining room give this area a spacious feeling. The side porch can be connected with a covered walk to the two-car detached garage, for which plans are included. The master bedroom has a ten-foot ceiling and a bay-windowed sitting area. Bedrooms 2 and 3 both have walk-in closets, while bedroom 3 offers a corner window seat.

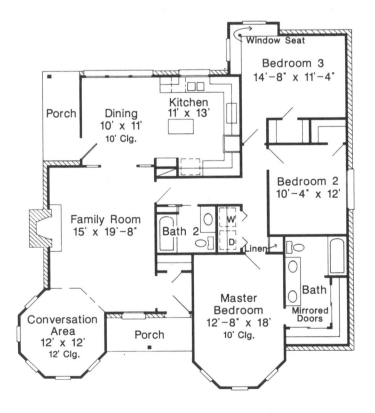

Window Seat

Bedroom 3
14'-8" x 11'-4"

Porch

Dining
10' x 11'
10' Clg.

Kitchen
11' x 13'

Bedroom 2
10'-4" x 12'

Family Room
15' x 19'-8"

Bath 2

W
D

Linen

Bath

Conversation
Area
12' x 12'
12' Clg.

Porch

Master
Bedroom
12'-8" x 18'
10' Clg.

Mirrored
Doors

8' Clg. Throughout
Unless Otherwise Noted

DESIGN M9050
BEDROOMS 3
BATHROOMS 2
SQUARE FOOTAGE 1,614
PRICE A1

WIDTH 45' 6"
DEPTH 47'

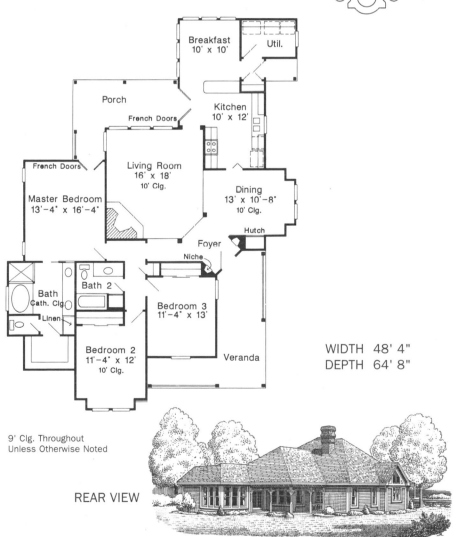

Breakfast
10' x 10'

Util.

Porch

French Doors

Kitchen
10' x 12'

French Doors

Living Room
16' x 18'
10' Clg.

Dining
13' x 10'-8"
10' Clg.

Master Bedroom
13'-4" x 16'-4"

Hutch

Foyer

Niche

Bath
Cath. Clg.

Bath 2

Linen

Bedroom 3
11'-4" x 13'

Bedroom 2
11'-4" x 12'
10' Clg.

Veranda

WIDTH 48' 4"
DEPTH 64' 8"

9' Clg. Throughout
Unless Otherwise Noted

REAR VIEW

The fine wood trim and copper roof at the box-bay window, along with the ornate fretwork and turned posts at the veranda, add a certain degree of elegance to this Queen Anne Style cottage. A leaded-glass front door opens to a foyer with built-in display niches on each side. The formal dining area has a ten-foot ceiling and built-in hutch. Four full-length windows offer an unobstructed view from the living area to the covered porch and rear yard. The kitchen overlooks a breakfast area with six large windows and a pair of French doors. The master bedroom also has French doors opening to the large rear porch. The master bath has a dramatic cathedral ceiling and a garden tub with angled glass windows above.

DESIGN M9052
BEDROOMS 3
BATHROOMS 2
SQUARE FOOTAGE 1,753
PRICE A4

VICTORIAN COTTAGE

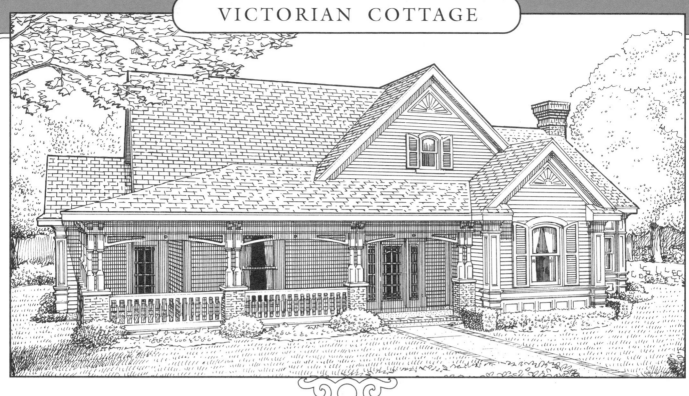

While much less elaborate than some other Victorian designs, the intersecting roof lines, arch-top windows with shutters, and detailed corner pilasters give this home a casual, yet distinctive appearance. An eight-foot-wide veranda provides plenty of room for outdoor entertaining. Inside, the large foyer opens to the formal dining area. A thirteen-foot raised ceiling with blocked panel trim and crown molding adds interest to the living room. French doors lead to a private library with built-in bookcases and a window seat. The secluded master suite offers a walk-in closet and an elegant bath with garden tub and glass-enclosed shower. Two large bedrooms each have walk-in closets and ceilings that slope from six feet to nine feet in height. Plans for a detached garage are included.

FIRST FLOOR

Linen
French Doors
Bath
Porch
French Door
Master Bedroom 14'-4" x 16'
Util.
Breakfast 10' x 9'
Kitchen 11'-4" x 11'-4"
French Door
Dining 11'-4" x 13'-4"
Living Room 17'-8" x 17' 13' Step-Up Clg.
Foyer
Porch
French Doors
Library 10'-8" x 11' 10' Clg.
Window Seat Books

SECOND FLOOR

Bedroom 2 12'-4" x 13'
6' Wall
6' Wall
Books
Balcony
Bedroom 3 11' x 14'
Bath 2
Linen

9' Clg. Throughout
First and Second Floor
Unless Otherwise Noted

DESIGN	M9008
BEDROOMS	3
BATHROOMS	2½
FIRST FLOOR	1,653 Sq. Ft.
SECOND FLOOR	613 Sq. Ft.
TOTAL	2,266 Sq. Ft.
PRICE	A4

GARAGE

WIDTH 54'
DEPTH 53' 8"

2-Car Garage

FIRST FLOOR

French Doors

Master Bedroom
13'-4" x 17'
11' Clg.

Bath

Breakfast
8' x 8'

Kitchen
16' x 12'

French Door

Bath 2

Util.

Bedroom 3
12' x 12'
11' Step-Up Clg.

Dining
15'-8" x 10'-8"
12' Clg.

Raised
Foyer

French
Doors

Bedroom 2
13' x 11'-4"

Living Room
21' x 14'-4"
12' Clg.

Veranda

SECOND FLOOR

Bath 3

Plant Shelves

Gameroom
18'-8" x 15'-4"

Foyer Below

9' Clg. Throughout
Unless Otherwise Noted

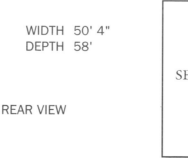

REAR VIEW

WIDTH 50' 4"
DEPTH 58'

A seven-foot wide veranda with ornate fretwork, porch railing and intricate post brackets, along with a copper-topped box window, provide this home with old-fashioned charm and romance. Inside, the raised foyer opens into the living and dining areas. Stairs lead to the second-floor game room and bath. Bedrooms 2 and 3 each have French doors that open to the front veranda. The secluded master bedroom has French doors, while the spacious master bath features a garden tub with adjacent glass-enclosed shower, along with a large walk-in closet. The kitchen has ample cabinet space, a center work island, and a magnificent view through the breakfast area to the rear yard. Plans for a detached two-car garage are included with this design.

DESIGN	M9030
BEDROOMS	3
BATHROOMS	3
FIRST FLOOR	1,837 Sq. Ft.
SECOND FLOOR	445 Sq. Ft.
TOTAL	2,282 Sq. Ft.
PRICE	A4

Elaborate spindlework and ornate porch posts, along with detailed block-paneled trim at the symmetrical gables, give this Queen Anne Style two-story charm and elegance. The living room has a fireplace as its focal point, while at the same time providing a view of the built-in media center. The large kitchen opens to the dining area, and also has access to the garage and laundry room. The master bedroom is truly a luxurious private retreat. The sitting area has a built-in media center for audio and video equipment. The master bath contains a glass-enclosed shower and His and Hers lavatories. Two additional bedrooms, each with a walk-in closet, share a hall bath.

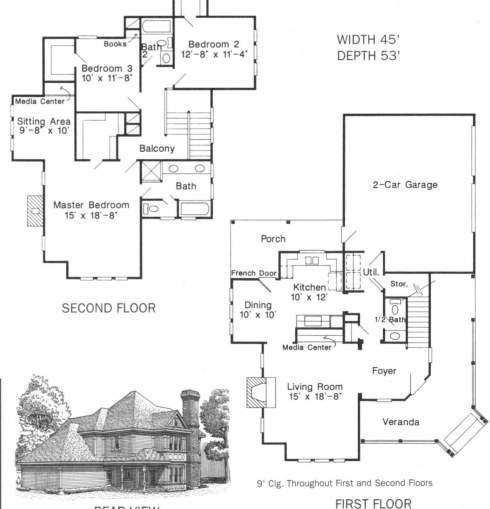

SECOND FLOOR

Books
Bath 2
Bedroom 2
12'-8" x 11'-4"
Bedroom 3
10' x 11'-8"
Media Center
Sitting Area
9'-8" x 10'
Balcony
Bath
Master Bedroom
15' x 18'-8"

WIDTH 45'
DEPTH 53'

2-Car Garage
Porch
French Door
Util.
Kitchen
10' x 12'
Stor.
Dining
10' x 10'
1/2 Bath
Media Center
Foyer
Living Room
15' x 18'-8"
Veranda

9' Clg. Throughout First and Second Floors

FIRST FLOOR

DESIGN	M9053
BEDROOMS	3
BATHROOMS	2½
FIRST FLOOR	811 Sq. Ft.
SECOND FLOOR	1,067 Sq. Ft.
TOTAL	1,878 Sq. Ft.
PRICE	A4

REAR VIEW

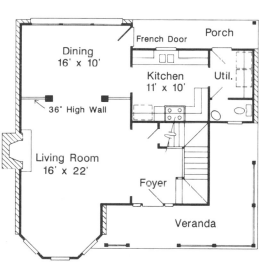

Dining
16' x 10'

French Door

Porch

Kitchen
11' x 10'

Util.

36" High Wall

FIRST FLOOR

Living Room
16' x 22'

Foyer

Veranda

9' Clg. Throughout First Floor

Bedrom 2
10' x 11'

Bath
2

Bedroom 3
10' x 12'

Bath
Cath. Clg.

Linen

Master
Bedroom
12' x 19'

Foyer
Below

WIDTH 37'
DEPTH 33' 10"

SECOND FLOOR

8' Clg. Throughout Second Floor

A steep-pitched roof, decorative shingles at the front gable, and a wraparound veranda accent this relatively economical Queen Anne Style design. Inside, an impressive foyer opens to the second-floor balcony. The living area is separated from the dining room with a half wall and paneled columns. An efficiently designed kitchen serves the dining room. The laundry room opens to the rear porch, which can be connected with a covered walk to the detached two-car garage, for which plans are included. Upstairs, leaded-glass windows fill the balcony and upper foyer with natural light. The master bedroom offers a walk-in closet, in addition to a mirrored closet in the bath area.

DESIGN	M9054
BEDROOMS	3
BATHROOMS	2½
FIRST FLOOR	860 Sq. Ft.
SECOND FLOOR	818 Sq. Ft.
TOTAL	1,678 Sq. Ft.
PRICE	A1

With its exceptional detail and proportions, this home is reminiscent of the Queen Anne Style. Turned posts resting on brick pedestals support a raised-gable entry to the veranda. The foyer opens to a living area with a bay-windowed alcove and a fireplace with flanking bookshelves. A large walk-in pantry and box window at the sink are special features in the kitchen. Natural light fills the breakfast area with a full-length bay window and a French door. Upstairs, the master bedroom offers unsurpassed elegance and convenience. The sitting area has an eleven-foot ceiling with arch-top windows. The bath area features a large walk-in closet, His and Hers lavatories, and plenty of linen storage. Plans for a two-car detached garage are included.

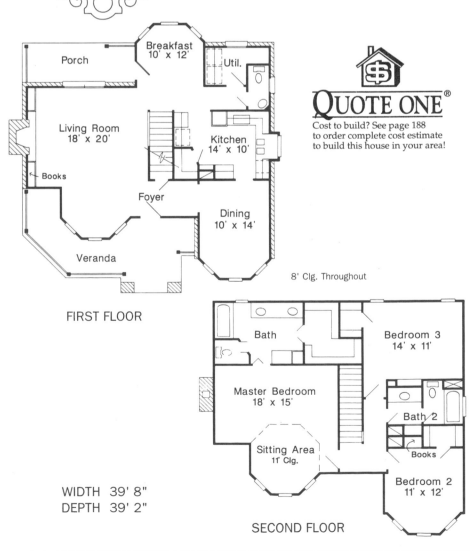

FIRST FLOOR

8' Clg. Throughout

SECOND FLOOR

WIDTH 39' 8"
DEPTH 39' 2"

DESIGN M9055
BEDROOMS 3
BATHROOMS 2½
FIRST FLOOR 997 Sq. Ft.
SECOND FLOOR 1,069 Sq. Ft.
TOTAL 2,066 Sq. Ft.
PRICE A5

Quote One®
Cost to build? See page 188 to order complete cost estimate to build this house in your area!

FIRST FLOOR

2-Car Garage

Porch

French Door

Breakfast
10' x 10'

Util.

Storage

Pantry

Media Center

Kitchen
16' x 10'

Family Room
18'-4" x 14'-8"

Desk Below
Landing

Seating

Study
12'-8" x 10'

Dining
11'-4" x 13'

Foyer

French Door

Living Room
14'-8" x 12'-8"

Arbor

Porch

First Floor

10' Clg. Throughout First Floor

Quote One®
Cost to build? See page 188
to order complete cost estimate
to build this house in your area!

SECOND FLOOR

Bedroom 4
12' x 11'

Bedroom 3
13' x 11'

Bath 3

32" High
Cabinet

Linen

Bath 2

Seat

Bedroom 2
12' x 13'

Bath

Linen

Alcove
10' x 7'

Master Bedroom
20'-4" x 14'-4"

9' Clg. Throughout Second Floor

WIDTH   46' 6"
DEPTH   65' 8"

Inside this charming turn-of-the-century design, classical columns separate the foyer and dining room. A French door opens from the living room to a lattice-covered side arbor. Double doors in both the living and family rooms provide access to a bay-windowed study with built-in bookcases and a desk. The large family room contains a fireplace, media cabinet, and a serving bar open from the kitchen. A six-foot curved picture window offers a full view of the rear porch from the breakfast and kitchen areas. Upstairs, the master suite features an elegant bath with a garden tub inset in a bay window, and a walk-in closet. Bedrooms 3 and 4 share a bath, while bedroom 2 has a private bath and a bay-windowed alcove.

DESIGN	M9056
BEDROOMS	4
BATHROOMS	3½
FIRST FLOOR	1,354 Sq. Ft.
SECOND FLOOR	1,418 Sq. Ft.
TOTAL	2,772 Sq. Ft.
PRICE	A4

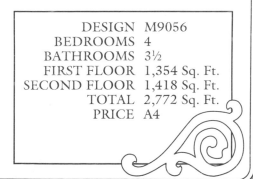

REAR VIEW

QUEEN ANNE

Classical columns on brick pedestals support a seven-foot veranda, beyond which extends an 11' x 18' lattice-covered arbor. In addition to a thirteen-foot vaulted ceiling, the dining room has French doors that open to both the rear yard and the front veranda. The living room has a bay window and two flanking windows. A breakfast alcove with expansive windows is part of the efficient kitchen. French doors and a bay window provide a comfortable retreat in the secluded master suite. Upstairs, the balcony overlooks a dramatic staircase and foyer below. Three additional bedrooms each have walk-in closets and special window treatments. The door of the attached two-car garage can be located at either side or to the rear.

DESIGN	M9009
BEDROOMS	4
BATHROOMS	2½
FIRST FLOOR	1,351 Sq. Ft.
SECOND FLOOR	862 Sq. Ft.
TOTAL	2,213 Sq. Ft.
PRICE	A4

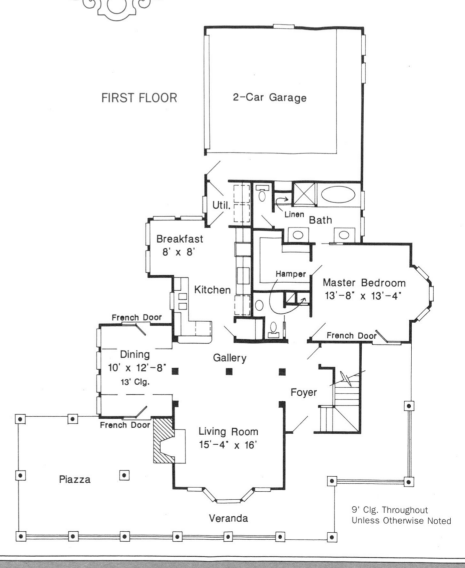

FIRST FLOOR

2-Car Garage

Util.

Linen

Bath

Breakfast 8' x 8'

Hamper

Master Bedroom 13'-8" x 13'-4"

Kitchen

French Door

Gallery

French Door

Dining 10' x 12'-8"
13' Clg.

Foyer

French Door

Living Room 15'-4" x 16'

Piazza

9' Clg. Throughout Unless Otherwise Noted

Veranda

REAR VIEW

WIDTH 46' 8"
WIDTH WITH PIAZZA 58' 4"
DEPTH 72' 4"

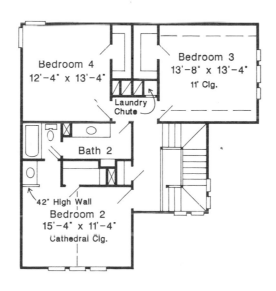

Bedroom 4
12'-4" x 13'-4"

Bedroom 3
13'-8" x 13'-4"
11' Clg.

Laundry
Chute

Bath 2

42" High Wall

Bedroom 2
15'-4" x 11'-4"
Cathedral Clg.

SECOND FLOOR

Queen Anne Victorians were the dominant style of homes during the last part of the 19th Century. Although the exterior of this home is more restrained than many of the typical Queen Anne examples, still present are the decorative front-facing gable, porch fretwork, and steeply pitched roof lines. Leaded-glass windows admit light into the spacious foyer, which is separated from the formal dining room by paneled columns. The private master suite includes a bay-windowed sitting room and spectacular bath. The kitchen overlooks a breakfast area with double French doors that open to a large rear porch. Upstairs, three bedrooms and a game room provide plenty of living space for a large family. Plans for a detached two-car garage are included.

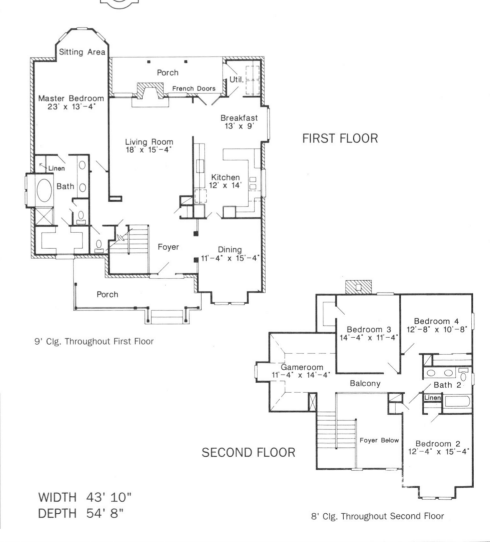

FIRST FLOOR

Sitting Area

Master Bedroom
23' x 13'-4"

Porch

French Doors

Util.

Living Room
18' x 15'-4"

Breakfast
13' x 9'

Linen

Bath

Kitchen
12' x 14'

Foyer

Dining
11'-4" x 15'-4"

Porch

9' Clg. Throughout First Floor

SECOND FLOOR

Bedroom 3
14'-4" x 11'-4"

Bedroom 4
12'-8" x 10'-8"

Gameroom
11'-4" x 14'-4"

Balcony

Bath 2

Linen

Foyer Below

Bedroom 2
12'-4" x 15'-4"

8' Clg. Throughout Second Floor

DESIGN M9057
BEDROOMS 4
BATHROOMS 2½
FIRST FLOOR 1,686 Sq. Ft.
SECOND FLOOR 965 Sq. Ft.
TOTAL 2,651 Sq. Ft.
PRICE A5

WIDTH 43' 10"
DEPTH 54' 8"

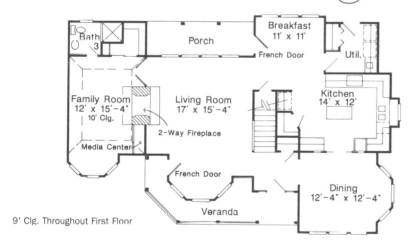

9' Clg. Throughout First Floor

FIRST FLOOR

8' Clg. Throughout Second Floor
Unless Otherwise Noted

SECOND FLOOR

WIDTH 52' 8"
DEPTH 33' 4"

Certainly, the most dominant feature of the Queen Anne Style is the tower at the front of the house. This design offers not only an octagon-shaped tower, but also ornate bay windows and decorative gable shingles. Inside, a two-way fireplace is functional in both the living room and family area. Highlights of the kitchen include a walk-in pantry, center work island, and box window at the sink. A French door opens from the breakfast room to a rear porch. The utility room leads to a detached two-car garage, for which the plans are included. Upstairs, the master bedroom is accented with a sitting area defined by a twelve-foot octagon-shaped ceiling. Two additional bedrooms share a dressing area and bath.

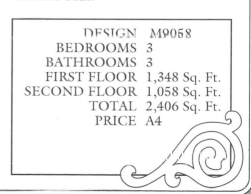

DESIGN   M9058
BEDROOMS   3
BATHROOMS   3
FIRST FLOOR   1,348 Sq. Ft.
SECOND FLOOR   1,058 Sq. Ft.
TOTAL   2,406 Sq. Ft.
PRICE   A4

With a veranda wrapping around an octagon-shaped turret, decorative shingle siding, and double posts placed on brick pedestals, this home recalls the grand Queen Anne Style designs of the late 19th Century. The foyer offers access to both the bay-windowed dining room and the living area. French doors lead from the living area to a game room, which can easily become a guest room with a private bath. The second floor features two children's bedrooms, each with a walk-in closet and built-in bookcase. The master bedroom has a sitting area with an eleven-foot-high octagon-shaped ceiling. Plenty of linen storage, along with a dressing table, combine with a separate glass-enclosed shower to create a superb master bath. Plans are included for a detached two-car garage.

FIRST FLOOR

8' Clg. Throughout
Unless Otherwise Noted

DESIGN	M9059
BEDROOMS	3
BATHROOMS	3
FIRST FLOOR	1,299 Sq. Ft.
SECOND FLOOR	1,069 Sq. Ft.
TOTAL	2,368 Sq. Ft.
PRICE	A2

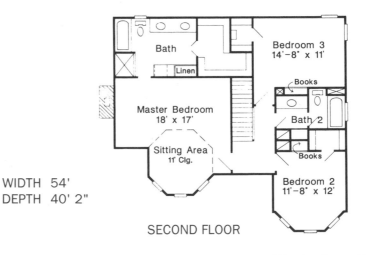

WIDTH 54'
DEPTH 40' 2"

SECOND FLOOR

FIRST FLOOR

Gameroom
12'-8" x 16'-8"

Bath 2

Porch

Breakfast
11'-4" x 11'

French Door

Util.

French Doors

Family Room
18' x 22'-4"

Kitchen
14' x 12'

8' Clg. Throughout
Unless Otherwise Noted

Foyer

Dining
10' x 11'

Veranda

SECOND FLOOR

Bath

Bedroom 3
10'-8" x 11'

Master Bedroom
18'-4" x 18'-8"

Books

Bath 3

Sitting Area
11' Clg.

Books

Books

Bedroom 2
11'-4" x 12'-8"

WIDTH 60'
DEPTH 44' 6"

The oval-glass front door of this elegant Queen Anne home opens into the foyer, which showcases the bannistered stairs. The spacious family room has a bay-windowed alcove and a fireplace. French doors lead to the game room, which can easily become guest quarters with a private bath. The kitchen offers a walk-in pantry and abundant cabinet and counter space. Adjacent to the bay-windowed breakfast room is a utility area, with room for the washer, dryer, freezer, and a small counter top with cabinets above. A door from this area can provide access to the two-car detached garage for which plans are included. Upstairs, bedrooms 2 and 3 each have walk-in closets, along with built-in bookcases. The master area, with its sitting alcove and special bath, is the perfect retreat.

DESIGN	M9060
BEDROOMS	3
BATHROOMS	3
FIRST FLOOR	1,326 Sq. Ft.
SECOND FLOOR	1,086 Sq. Ft.
TOTAL	2,412 Sq. Ft.
PRICE	A2

Double doors open from the two-story foyer to a private study with built-in bookcases and a bay window. The gallery, with decorative wood columns and an arched ceiling, overlooks both the large formal dining and living rooms. French doors open from the living room to the front veranda and the screened porch. A fireplace adds warmth to the breakfast area and the island kitchen. A twelve-foot octagon-shaped ceiling and leaded-glass windows define a cozy sitting area in the master suite. The dressing area, with His and Hers walk-in closets, leads to a luxurious bath. An optional exercise loft and plant shelves complete this elegant master bath. Two additional bedrooms, one with a private deck, share a dressing area and bath.

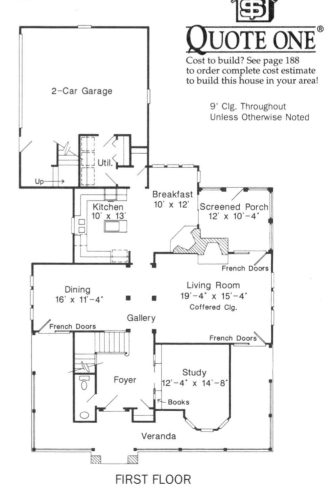

Quote One®
Cost to build? See page 188
to order complete cost estimate
to build this house in your area!

9' Clg. Throughout
Unless Otherwise Noted

2-Car Garage

Util.

Up

Kitchen
10' x 13'

Breakfast
10' x 12'

Screened Porch
12' x 10'-4"

French Doors

Dining
16' x 11'-4"

Living Room
19'-4" x 15'-4"
Coffered Clg.

Gallery

French Doors

French Doors

Foyer

Study
12'-4" x 14'-8"

Books

Veranda

FIRST FLOOR

DESIGN	M9012
BEDROOMS	3
BATHROOMS	2½
FIRST FLOOR	1,357 Sq. Ft.
SECOND FLOOR	1,079 Sq. Ft.
TOTAL	2,436 Sq. Ft.
PRICE	A4

WIDTH 42' 8"
DEPTH 75'

REAR VIEW

Office
16'-4" x 17'

Optional Second Floor
At Garage
167 Sq. Ft.

Incline Ladder — Bath Below

Exercise Loft
15 x 13

Optional Exercise Loft
228 Sq. Ft.

SECOND FLOOR

Deck

French Doors

Bedroom 2
12' x 11'-4"

Bath 2

Up

Bath

Bedroom 3
12' x 11'-4"
Cathedral Clg.

Foyer
Below

Master Bedroom
12'-4" x 15'

Seat
Books

Balcony

Sitting
Area
12' Clg.

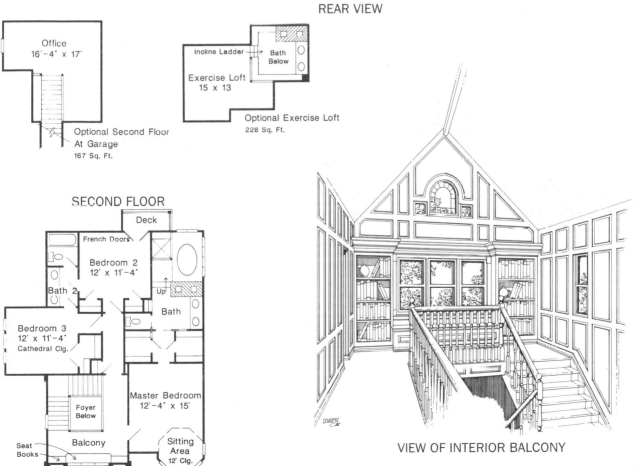

VIEW OF INTERIOR BALCONY

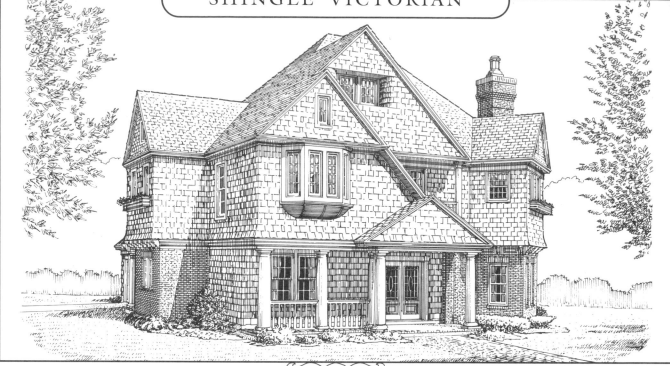

The double leaded-glass doors of this Shingle Style design open into an elegant foyer. The study features raised-panel walls, built-in bookcases and a fireplace. Overlooking the breakfast area and the living room is a spacious kitchen with a walk-in pantry and island cooktop. The living room contains a built-in media center, French doors to the rear porch, and a refreshment bar. Upstairs, the secluded master suite offers a windowed alcove and access to the covered front balcony. The elegant bath utilizes glass block walls for the shower and water closet areas. A corner garden tub and a large walk-in closet complete this area. The additional bedrooms each have unique bay windows and private lavatories.

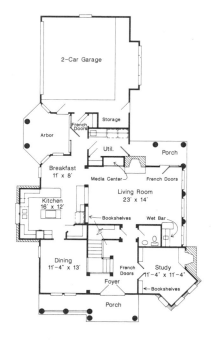

FIRST FLOOR

SECOND FLOOR

9' Clg. Throughout
Unless Otherwise Noted

DESIGN M9010
BEDROOMS 3
BATHROOMS 2½
FIRST FLOOR 1,401 Sq. Ft.
SECOND FLOOR 1,189 Sq. Ft.
TOTAL 2,590 Sq. Ft.
PRICE A4

RIGHT SIDE VIEW

WIDTH 44' 8"
DEPTH 75' 4"

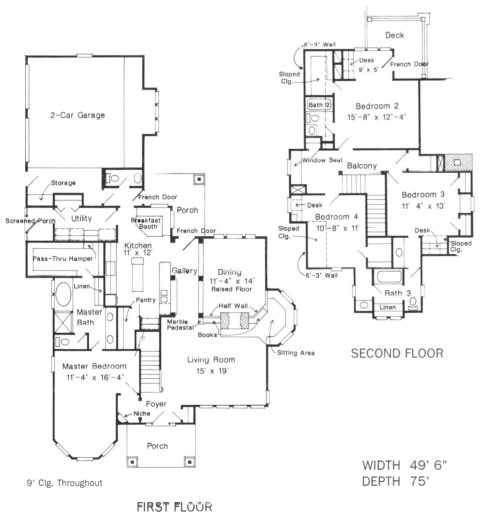

SECOND FLOOR

Deck

6'-3" Wall

Desk
9' x 5'

French Door

Sloped Clg.

Bath 2

Bedroom 2
15'-8" x 12'-4"

Window Seat

Balcony

Bedroom 3
11' 4' x 13'

Desk

Bedroom 4
10'-8" x 11'

Sloped Clg.

Desk

Sloped Clg.

6'-3" Wall

Bath 3

Linen

2-Car Garage

Storage

French Door

Porch

Screened Porch

Utility

Breakfast Booth

French Door

Pass-Thru Hamper

Kitchen
11' x 12'

Gallery

Dining
11'-4" x 14'
Raised Floor

Linen

Pantry

Master Bath

Half Wall

Marble Pedestal

Books

Master Bedroom
11'-4" x 16'-4"

Living Room
15' x 19'

Sitting Area

Foyer

Niche

Porch

9' Clg. Throughout

FIRST FLOOR

WIDTH 49' 6"
DEPTH 75'

Designed to maximize views to the front, side, and rear outdoor areas, this home utilizes strategically placed windows and an open floor plan. The two-way fireplace and half wall with built-in bookcases separate the living and dining areas. A center work island and walk-in pantry, along with a built-in breakfast nook, are special kitchen amenities. The master suite provides a comfortable retreat with a bay-windowed sitting area and a magnificent bath. Upstairs, a large balcony with a window seat leads to three additional bedrooms. Bedrooms 3 and 4 each feature built-in desks and private dressing areas. Bedroom 2 has a private bath, built-in desk, and French door opening to a rear deck.

DESIGN	M9011
BEDROOMS	4
BATHROOMS	3½
FIRST FLOOR	1,637 Sq. Ft.
SECOND FLOOR	1,062 Sq. Ft.
TOTAL	2,699 Sq. Ft.
PRICE	A4

Reminiscent of the grand brick Victorians of the late 19th Century, this design features a raised octagon-shaped turret with wraparound veranda, and patterned shingle siding at the gables. The large, two-story living room is perfect for formal or family entertaining, with the breakfast area and kitchen close by. A study with built-in bookcases is perfect for a home office or relaxing reading area. The master suite has a sitting area and a luxurious bath with a glass-enclosed shower, linen storage, and a walk-in closet with full-length mirrored doors. Each of the three upstairs bedrooms has a private lavatory area and ample closet space. The large game room features a cathedral ceiling and a balcony railing overlooking the living room.

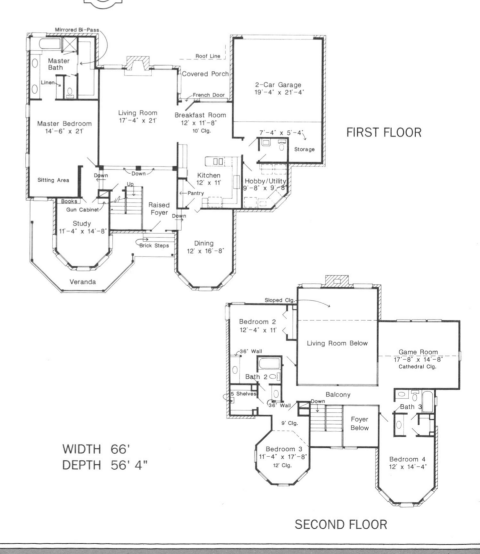

FIRST FLOOR

WIDTH 66'
DEPTH 56' 4"

SECOND FLOOR

DESIGN	M9061
BEDROOMS	4
BATHROOMS	3½
FIRST FLOOR	2,087 Sq. Ft.
SECOND FLOOR	1,150 Sq. Ft.
TOTAL	3,237 Sq. Ft.
PRICE	A3

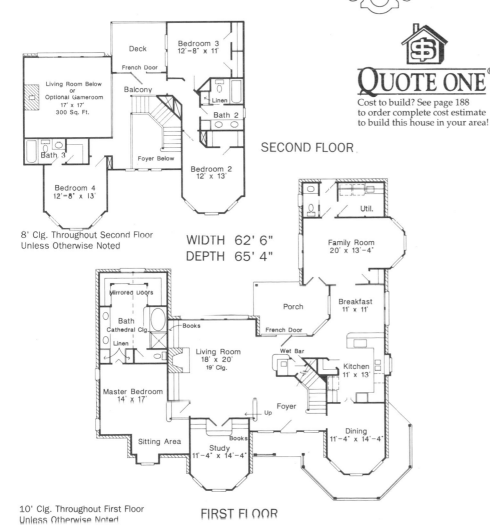

Deck

Bedroom 3
12'-8" x 11'

French Door

Living Room Below
or
Optional Gameroom
17' x 17'
300 Sq. Ft.

Balcony

Linen

Bath 2

Bath 3

Foyer Below

Bedroom 2
12' x 13'

Bedroom 4
12'-8" x 13'

SECOND FLOOR

8' Clg. Throughout Second Floor
Unless Otherwise Noted

WIDTH 62' 6"
DEPTH 65' 4"

Util.

Family Room
20' x 13'-4"

Mirrored Doors

Bath
Cathedral Clg.

Books

Linen

Porch

Breakfast
11' x 11'

French Door

Wet Bar

Living Room
18' x 20'
19' Clg.

Kitchen
11' x 13'

Master Bedroom
14' x 17'

Foyer

Up

Sitting Area

Books

Study
11'-4" x 14'-4"

Dining
11'-4" x 14'-4"

10' Clg. Throughout First Floor
Unless Otherwise Noted

FIRST FLOOR

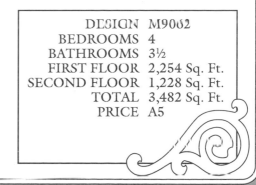

QUOTE ONE®

Cost to build? See page 188
to order complete cost estimate
to build this house in your area!

Decorative shingle siding and a
dominant front veranda create a
charming turn-of-the-century exterior.
The magnificent foyer offers a view of
the two-story living area with floor-to-
ceiling glass at the rear. A raised
walkway provides a dramatic entry to
the master suite with a cozy sitting
area. The kitchen features a walk-in
pantry and boxed-out window at the
sink. The family room has a bay-
window area and French doors
opening to the covered porch. A
hallway leads to a two-car detached
garage, for which plans are included.
Upstairs, a balcony walkway leads to
bedroom 4 with a private bath.
Bedrooms 2 and 3 have ample closet
space and a shared bath with separate
dressing areas. The plans offer an
optional 17' x 17' game area above
the living room.

DESIGN	M9062
BEDROOMS	4
BATHROOMS	3½
FIRST FLOOR	2,254 Sq. Ft.
SECOND FLOOR	1,228 Sq. Ft.
TOTAL	3,482 Sq. Ft.
PRICE	A5

The living area of this spectacular Queen Anne Style home features a fireplace and a bay-windowed alcove. The centrally located kitchen overlooks a dining area with full-length windows and a French door. The master bedroom has a large walk-in closet and French doors opening to the rear veranda. The master bath provides additional closet space, along with a glass-enclosed shower and an oval tub in an octagon-shaped alcove. Upstairs, French doors open into a game room. Bedroom 2 has a walk-in closet and a ten-foot sloped ceiling. Bedroom 3 also has a walk-in closet and a raised octagon-shaped ceiling. Plans are included for a detached two-car garage and an optional screened porch.

Quote One®
Cost to build? See page 188 to order complete cost estimate to build this house in your area!

WIDTH 40' 4"
DEPTH 62' 10"

8' Clg. Throughout Second Floor
Unless Otherwise Noted

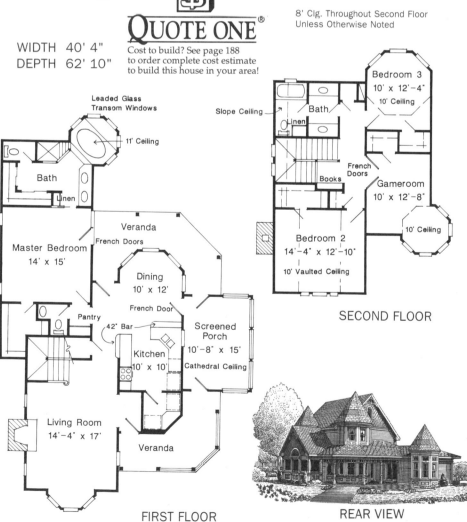

SECOND FLOOR

FIRST FLOOR

REAR VIEW

DESIGN M9063
BEDROOMS 3
BATHROOMS 2½
FIRST FLOOR 1,236 Sq. Ft.
SECOND FLOOR 835 Sq. Ft.
TOTAL 2,071 Sq. Ft.
PRICE A4

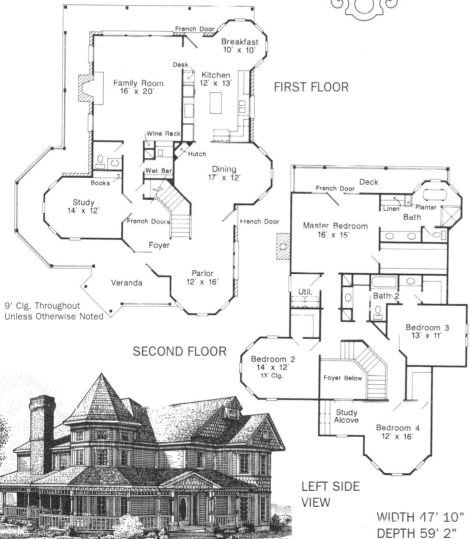

French Door

Breakfast
10' x 10'

Desk

Family Room
16' x 20'

Kitchen
12' x 13'

FIRST FLOOR

Wine Rack

Hutch

Wet Bar

Dining
17' x 12'

Books

Study
14' x 12'

French Doors

French Door

Foyer

Veranda

Parlor
12' x 16'

9' Clg. Throughout
Unless Otherwise Noted

Deck

French Door

Linen

Planter

Bath

Master Bedroom
16' x 15'

Util.

Bath 2

Bedroom 3
13' x 11'

SECOND FLOOR

Bedroom 2
14' x 12'
13' Clg.

Foyer Below

Study
Alcove

Bedroom 4
12' x 16'

The angled entry opens to a grand foyer and a formal parlor with expansive windows and a French door leading to the side yard. Double French doors open from the foyer to the large study with bookcases and full-length windows. The spacious family room features a fireplace and a wet bar. The kitchen, with a work island and abundant cabinet space, overlooks the octagon-shaped breakfast room. Upstairs, the master bedroom has French doors which open onto a rear deck. Three additional bedrooms each have walk-in closets. Bedroom 2 has a thirteen-foot octagon-shaped ceiling, while bedroom 4 offers a cozy alcove with built-in desk and shuttered opening to the foyer. Plans for a two-car detached garage are included.

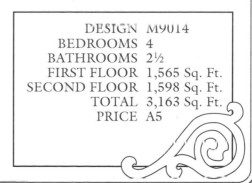

LEFT SIDE VIEW

WIDTH 47' 10"
DEPTH 59' 2"

DESIGN M9014
BEDROOMS 4
BATHROOMS 2½
FIRST FLOOR 1,565 Sq. Ft.
SECOND FLOOR 1,598 Sq. Ft.
TOTAL 3,163 Sq. Ft.
PRICE A5

QUEEN ANNE

An oval-glass front door with side-lights opens into a raised foyer, which overlooks the formal dining and living areas. The bookcase-lined alcove at the front of the living room is a perfect reading area. The kitchen features a walk-in pantry, center island with vegetable sink, and an abundance of counter and cabinet space. The master retreat features a special bath with glass-enclosed shower, oval tub, and a dressing alcove with mirrored closet doors. The centrally located staircase is both elegant and practical. Upstairs, bedrooms 3 and 4 offer private lavatory areas, while sharing a bath. Bedroom 2 has a personal bath, walk-in closet and built-in desk. The balcony has three leaded-glass windows above a window seat.

DESIGN	M9064
BEDROOMS	4
BATHROOMS	3½
FIRST FLOOR	2,114 Sq. Ft.
SECOND FLOOR	942 Sq. Ft.
TOTAL	3,056 Sq. Ft.
PRICE	A3

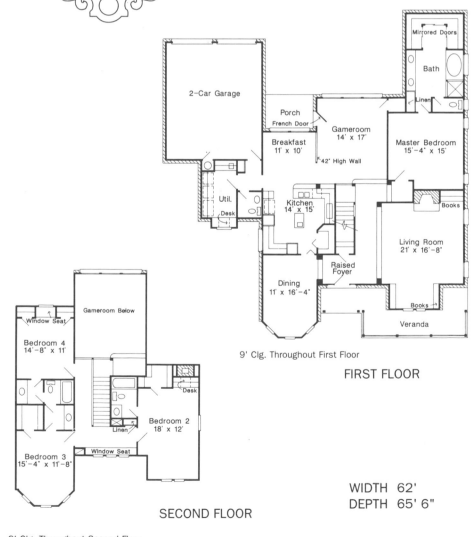

9' Clg. Throughout First Floor

FIRST FLOOR

SECOND FLOOR

8' Clg. Throughout Second Floor

WIDTH 62'
DEPTH 65' 6"

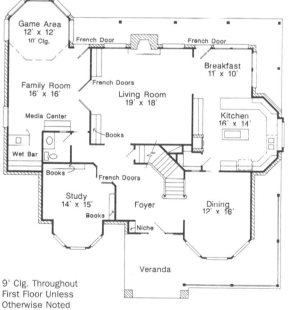

Game Area 12' x 12' 10' Clg.

French Door   French Door

Breakfast 11' x 10'

Family Room 16' x 16'

French Doors

Living Room 19' x 18'

Kitchen 16' x 14'

Media Center

Books

Wet Bar

Books

French Doors

Study 14' x 15'

Foyer

Dining 12' x 16'

Books

Niche

Veranda

FIRST FLOOR

9' Clg. Throughout First Floor Unless Otherwise Noted

8' Clg. Throughout Second Floor Unless Otherwise Noted

The dramatic two-story foyer leads to the study and living room, both with built-in cabinets and bookcases. The family room features a game table area with full-length windows, along with a wet bar and media center. The kitchen is a gourmet's delight with an island cooktop, walk-in pantry, and an oven inset in brick. French doors open onto the rear porch from the breakfast area and the family room. Upstairs, bedrooms 2 and 3 each have walk-in closets and private dressing areas. A ten-foot octagon-shaped ceiling and leaded-glass windows define a cozy sitting area in the master suite. A two-car detached garage design is included in the plans.

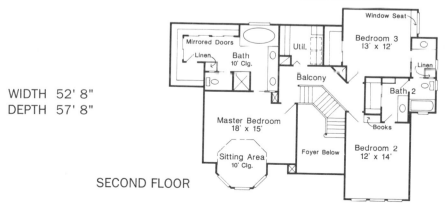

WIDTH 52' 8"
DEPTH 57' 8"

Mirrored Doors

Linen

Bath 10' Clg.

Util.

Window Seat

Bedroom 3 13' x 12'

Linen

Balcony

Bath 2

Master Bedroom 18' x 15'

Books

Foyer Below

Bedroom 2 12' x 14'

Sitting Area 10' Clg.

SECOND FLOOR

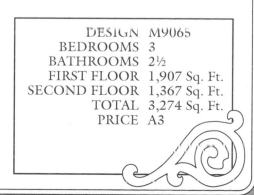

DESIGN	M9065
BEDROOMS	3
BATHROOMS	2½
FIRST FLOOR	1,907 Sq. Ft.
SECOND FLOOR	1,367 Sq. Ft.
TOTAL	3,274 Sq. Ft.
PRICE	A3

9' Clg. Throughout Unless Otherwise Noted

The leaded-glass front door opens into a spacious foyer, which offers a view of the formal dining room. The living room features a fireplace with cabinets on one side and a window seat on the other. A library alcove, with windows above a desk and a four-foot bookcase below the stairs, connects the living and family areas. The kitchen features an island cooktop, an angled window and sink, and a French door leading to the side veranda. Adjacent to the kitchen is a staircase to an optional game room or living quarters. The master suite offers a private media center with built-in seating and cabinets for audio and video equipment. The two additional bedrooms each have closets and private bathrooms.

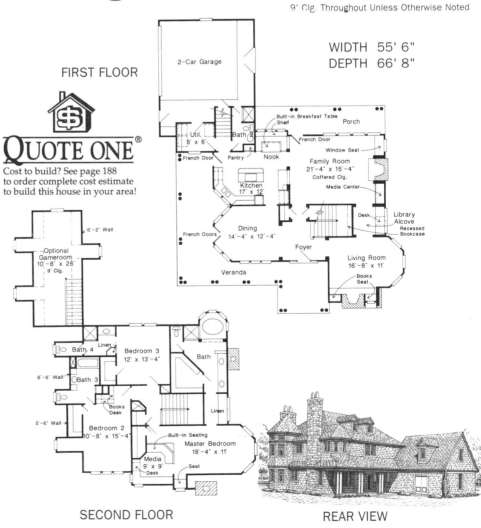

FIRST FLOOR

QUOTE ONE®

Cost to build? See page 188 to order complete cost estimate to build this house in your area!

WIDTH 55' 6"
DEPTH 66' 8"

SECOND FLOOR

REAR VIEW

DESIGN	M9066
BEDROOMS	3
BATHROOMS	4
FIRST FLOOR	1,353 Sq. Ft.
SECOND FLOOR	1,279 Sq. Ft.
GAME ROOM (OPTIONAL)	311 Sq. Ft.
TOTAL	2,943 Sq. Ft.
PRICE	A4

FOLK VICTORIAN

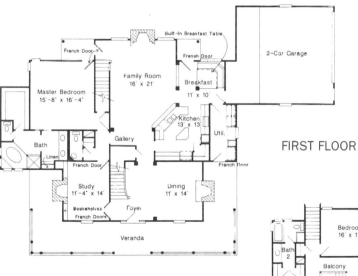

FIRST FLOOR

9' Clg. Throughout

French Door
Family Room
16' x 21'
Built-In Breakfast Table
French Door
Breakfast
11' x 10'
2-Car Garage
Master Bedroom
15'-8" x 16'-4"
Kitchen
13' x 13'
Util.
Bath
Gallery
Linen
French Door
French Door
Study
11'-4" x 14'
Dining
11' x 14'
Bookshelves
French Doors
Foyer
Veranda

SECOND FLOOR

Bath 2
Bedroom 4
16' x 11'-4"
Bath 3
Balcony
Bedroom 2
11'-4" x 16'
Foyer Below
Bedroom 3
11'-4" x 15'
Desk

The wraparound veranda and simple lines give this home an unassuming elegance that is characteristic of its Folk Victorian heritage. Opening directly to the formal dining room, the two-story foyer offers extra space for large dinner parties. French doors lead to the study with a cozy fireplace. The private master suite features a corner garden tub, glass-enclosed shower, and a walk-in closet. Overlooking the family room and built-in breakfast nook is the central kitchen. A rear staircase provides convenient access to the second floor from the family room. The balcony provides a view of the foyer below and the Palladian window. Three additional bedrooms complete this exquisite home.

DESIGN	M9067
BEDROOMS	4
BATHROOMS	3½
FIRST FLOOR	1,999 Sq. Ft.
SECOND FLOOR	933 Sq. Ft.
TOTAL	2,932 Sq. Ft.
PRICE	A4

WIDTH 79' 8"
DEPTH 59'

REAR VIEW

The raised turret with a wraparound veranda and front gable with decorative shingle siding dominate the facade of this Queen Anne Style home. An alcove is situated at the front of the living room. The country-style kitchen opens directly to the breakfast area. The secluded master bedroom features a master bath with His and Hers walk-in closets, a custom octagon-shaped tub and separate shower. A rear door at the utility room opens to the back porch, which can be connected with an optional covered walk to the detached two-car garage, for which plans are included. Upstairs, three bedrooms share a large, well-planned bathroom.

WIDTH 59' 8"
DEPTH 57' 8"

8' Clg. Throughout
Second Floor
Unless Otherwise Noted

SECOND FLOOR

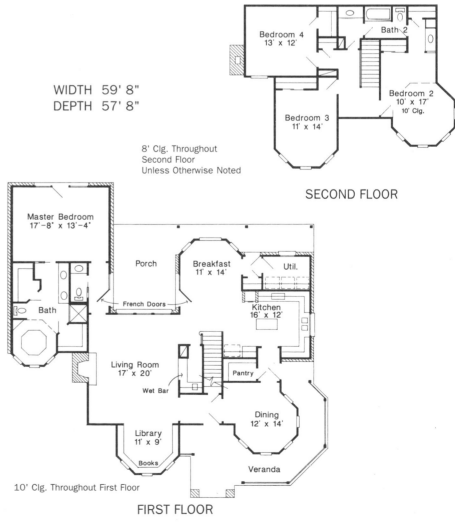

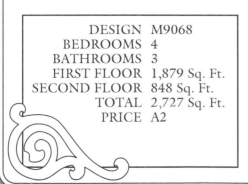

DESIGN M9068
BEDROOMS 4
BATHROOMS 3
FIRST FLOOR 1,879 Sq. Ft.
SECOND FLOOR 848 Sq. Ft.
TOTAL 2,727 Sq. Ft.
PRICE A2

10' Clg. Throughout First Floor

FIRST FLOOR

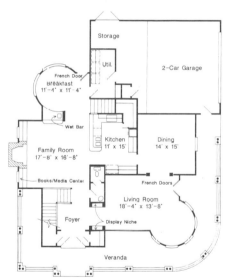

FIRST FLOOR

Storage

Util.

2-Car Garage

French Door
Breakfast
11'-4" x 11'-4"

Wet Bar

Kitchen
11' x 15'

Dining
14' x 15'

Family Room
17'-8" x 16'-8"

Books/Media Center

French Doors

Living Room
18'-4" x 13'-8"

Foyer

Display Niche

Veranda

Optional
Loft
12' x 11'-4"
136 Sq. Ft.

9' Clg. Throughout
Unless Otherwise Noted

REAR VIEW

QUOTE ONE®

Cost to build? See page 188
to order complete cost estimate
to build this house in your area!

Bedroom 2
12' x 15'
Cathedral Clg.

Linen
Bath 2

Bath 3

Bedroom 3
11'-8" x 11'-8"

Balcony

Linen

Bedroom 4
12' x 16'-8"

Bath

Bath 4

Barrel Clg.
Above Bath

Up To Optional
Exercise Room

Sauna

Master Bedroom
18'-4" x 13'-8"

Balcony

Foyer
Below

Sitting Area
11'-4" x 11'-4"
Vaulted Clg.

Balcony

SECOND FLOOR

Queen Anne Style homes of the late 19th Century feature some of the most elaborate and intricate construction and detailing ever witnessed in residential design. Reminiscent of these grand homes, this design offers some of the same distinctive characteristics: the patterned shingle siding, ornate spindlework, porch balustrades and the curved windows in the raised turrets. Leaded-glass doors open to a truly grand foyer with elegant staircase to a balcony above. The living room has a sitting area and French doors to a side veranda. Upstairs is the private master suite with luxurious bath, and three additional bedrooms, each with private bath and walk-in closet.

DESIGN	M9017
BEDROOMS	4
BATHROOMS	4½
FIRST FLOOR	1,617 Sq. Ft.
SECOND FLOOR	1,818 Sq. Ft.
OPTIONAL LOFT	136 Sq. Ft.
TOTAL	3,435 Sq. Ft.
PRICE	A5

WIDTH 53'
DEPTH 64' 8"

This home offers the essential characteristics of the Queen Anne Style—a raised turret and ornate spindlework at the veranda—but adds the practicality of a brick-veneer first floor. Inside, the living room has a bay-windowed alcove and a massive brick fireplace. Full-length windows on two sides of the breakfast room offer an expansive view of the rear yard. Matching sets of French doors open from the gallery and the master bedroom to the porch. An optional two-way fireplace separates the master bedroom and bath. Upstairs, bedrooms 3 and 4 each have private lavatories and walk-in closets. The game room has an optional fireplace and wet bar. Plans for a two-car detached garage are included.

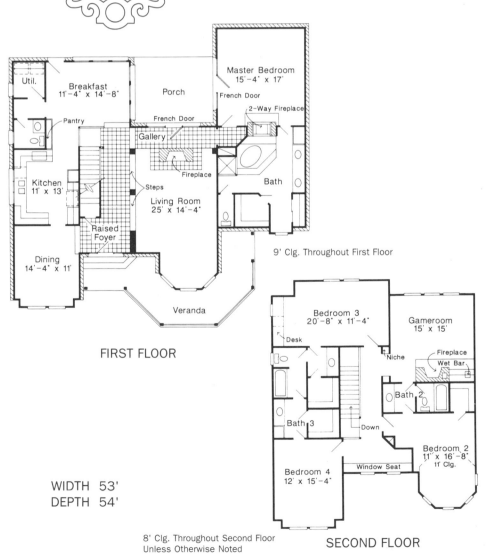

FIRST FLOOR

9' Clg. Throughout First Floor

8' Clg. Throughout Second Floor
Unless Otherwise Noted

SECOND FLOOR

DESIGN M9069
BEDROOMS 4
BATHROOMS 3½
FIRST FLOOR 1,937 Sq. Ft.
SECOND FLOOR 1,410 Sq. Ft.
TOTAL 3,347 Sq. Ft.
PRICE A5

WIDTH 53'
DEPTH 54'

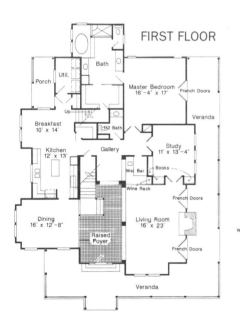

FIRST FLOOR

Bath
Porch
Util.
Up
Master Bedroom
16'-4" x 17'
French Doors
Veranda
Breakfast
10' x 14'
1½ Bath
Kitchen
12' x 13'
Gallery
Study
11' x 13'-4'
Wet Bar
Books
Wine Rack
French Doors
Dining
16' x 12'-8"
Raised Foyer
Living Room
16' x 23'
French Doors
French Doors
Veranda

WIDTH 54' 4"
DEPTH 75'

10' Clg. Throughout First Floor

8' Clg. Throughout Second Floor

Plant Shelf
Bedroom 2
15' x 10'
Balcony
Bath 3
Bedroom 3
13' x 15'-4'
Window Seats
Bath 2
Media Center
Up To Optional Third Floor
Bedroom 4
13' x 13'
Foyer Below
Gameroom
16' x 23'

SECOND FLOOR

**LEFT
SIDE VIEW**

This Victorian-inspired home, with its wide veranda and generous use of expansive windows and French doors, can take advantage of a building site that offers views in every direction. The raised foyer directly overlooks the formal dining room and the living area. Special features like the built-in bookcases in the study, the wet bar serving both living area and gallery, and an island kitchen with attached breakfast room and walk-in pantry make the gathering and working areas complete. Note the spacious bed rooms—master with whirlpool bath on the first floor and three additional bedrooms upstairs. Also upstairs is a game room with media center and fireplace. A staircase leads to an optional third-floor area. A two-car detached garage plan is included with this design.

DESIGN	M9013
BEDROOMS	4
BATHROOMS	3½
FIRST FLOOR	2,385 Sq. Ft.
SECOND FLOOR	1,467 Sq. Ft.
TOTAL	3,852 Sq. Ft.
PRICE	A5

SHINGLE VICTORIAN

Towards the end of the Victorian era, a new style began to emerge along the Eastern Seaboard. Later referred to as the Shingle Style, these new designs were influenced by the Colonial Revival and Queen Anne homes. Often incorporating diverse architectural elements, the shingle siding is one of the common elements of this style. With its cantilevered gable sloping in a gentle curve to the first floor, and a raised turret, this design is representative of this late 19th-Century style. Besides the living and dining rooms with coffered ceilings, the home boasts a study with curved walls, central gallery and family room with sunken media center. The island kitchen has an adjacent breakfast booth. Upstairs is a grand master suite and three additional bedrooms.

FIRST FLOOR

SECOND FLOOR

9' Clg. Throughout Unless Otherwise Noted

DESIGN	M9016
BEDROOMS	4
BATHROOMS	4½
FIRST FLOOR	1,812 Sq. Ft.
SECOND FLOOR	1,997 Sq. Ft.
TOTAL	3,809 Sq. Ft.
PRICE	A5

WIDTH 49' 2"
DEPTH 71' 8"

REAR VIEW

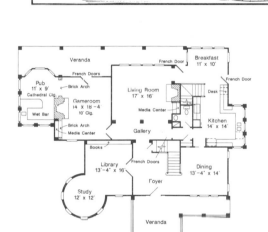

FIRST FLOOR

9' Clg. Throughout First and Second Floor
Unless Otherwise Noted

SECOND FLOOR

WIDTH 65' 4"
DEPTH 56'

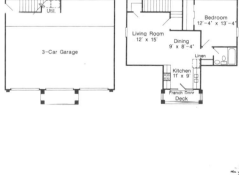

**DETACHED
3-CAR GARAGE**

Reminiscent of the fashionable summer homes of Newport, Cape Cod, this home typifies the Shingle Style with its wide verandas, shingled surfaces, Palladian window, and circular tower. The library features a built-in bookcase and circular study. To the left of the fireplace in the game room is a brick archway with built-in media center. To the right, a matching brick archway leads to the adjoining pub and walk-in wet bar. Windows surround the spacious kitchen. The second-floor master suite includes two oversized walk-in closets and a luxury bath. Three additional bedrooms and two baths, as well as a multi-purpose media room, are also on the second floor. Plans for a three-car detached garage with second-floor living quarters are included.

DESIGN M9070
BEDROOMS 4
BATHROOMS 4½
FIRST FLOOR 2,083 Sq. Ft.
SECOND FLOOR 1,938 Sq. Ft.
TOTAL 4,021 Sq. Ft.
PRICE A6

This lovely Queen Anne Style design has all the amenities you would expect in such a grand home. The raised foyer overlooks the formal dining room and living area, and provides access to a bay-windowed study and the secluded master suite with a sitting area, fireplace, and amenity-laden bath. Next to the large kitchen and breakfast area is a laundry room, and a special home office or hobby room. Upstairs, bedrooms 2 and 3 each have walk-in closets and separate dressing areas. Bedroom 4 features a built-in desk and a private dressing area. Triple French doors open from the balcony to a spectacular game room. Plans for a two-car detached garage are included.

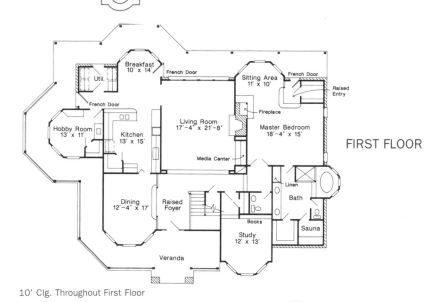

FIRST FLOOR

- Breakfast 10' x 14'
- French Door
- Util.
- French Door
- Sitting Area 11' x 10'
- French Door
- Raised Entry
- Fireplace
- Hobby Room 13' x 11'
- Kitchen 13' x 15'
- Living Room 17'-4" x 21'-8"
- Master Bedroom 18'-4" x 15'
- Media Center
- Linen
- Bath
- Dining 12'-4" x 17'
- Raised Foyer
- Books
- Sauna
- Study 12' x 13'
- Veranda

10' Clg. Throughout First Floor

SECOND FLOOR

- Window Seat
- Gameroom 15'-4" x 14'-8"
- Stor.
- French Door
- Living Room Below
- Game Alcove 13' x 11' 10' Clg.
- Bath 3
- Bedroom 2 12'-4" x 15'
- Desk
- Balcony
- Bedroom 4 12'-4" x 17' 11' Clg.
- Foyer Below
- Bath 2
- Bedroom 3 12' x 14'

8' Clg. Throughout Second Floor Unless Otherwise Noted

DESIGN	M9071
BEDROOMS	4
BATHROOMS	3½
FIRST FLOOR	2,524 Sq. Ft.
SECOND FLOOR	1,529 Sq. Ft.
TOTAL	4,053 Sq. Ft.
PRICE	A5

WIDTH 75' 8"
DEPTH 62' 4"

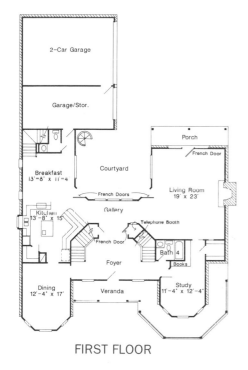

FIRST FLOOR

8' Clg. Throughout
Unless Otherwise Noted

WIDTH 53' 6"
DEPTH 82' 8"

Balance and symmetry, along with elaborate gingerbread detailing, highlight this Queen Anne Style design. Inside, the living room, kitchen, and breakfast area are ideal for relaxing or entertaining. Accessible from the foyer and living room, the study has a walk-in storage area, and built-in bookcases. It can double as a guest room. From the breakfast area, rear stairs lead to the second floor. Bedroom 3 can be a secluded area for an older child. The conveniently located utility room not only offers plenty of space for the laundry, but also has room for various other hobbies or projects. Leading to the master suite is a balcony that overlooks the dramatic foyer and stairs on one side, and the courtyard on the other.

SECOND FLOOR

DESIGN	M9072
BEDROOMS	3
BATHROOMS	4½
FIRST FLOOR	1,920 Sq. Ft.
SECOND FLOOR	1,898 Sq. Ft.
TOTAL	3,818 Sq. Ft.
PRICE	A3

All of the essential elements of the Queen Anne Style are present on the exterior of this gracious and inviting home. However, once inside, it immediately becomes obvious that this design reflects the lifestyles of today. The living room features built-in bookcases and a media center, and an expansive window treatment. The optional garden room can be fully enclosed for all-weather enjoyment, or left open as a covered porch. The island kitchen overlooks a bay-windowed breakfast area. The master suite has a sitting alcove with leaded-glass transom window. An enormous bath showcases an oversized garden tub. Upstairs, bedrooms 3 and 4 share a large bath. The game room has an optional fireplace and built-in bookcases and media cabinets.

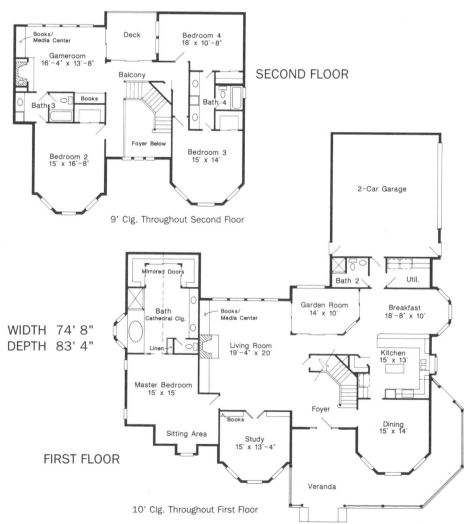

WIDTH 74' 8"
DEPTH 83' 4"

SECOND FLOOR

9' Clg. Throughout Second Floor

FIRST FLOOR

10' Clg. Throughout First Floor

DESIGN M9073
BEDROOMS 4
BATHROOMS 4
FIRST FLOOR 2,609 Sq. Ft.
SECOND FLOOR 1,482 Sq. Ft.
TOTAL 4,091 Sq. Ft.
PRICE A5

FOLK VICTORIAN

FIRST FLOOR

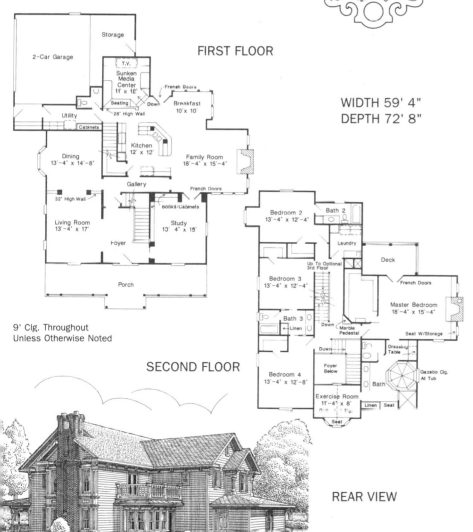

Storage

2-Car Garage

T.V.
Sunken Media Center
11' x 12'

French Doors

Seating
28" High Wall

Down

Breakfast
10' x 10'

Utility

Cabinets

Dining
13'-4" x 14'-8'

Kitchen
12' x 12'

Family Room
18'-4" x 15'-4"

Gallery

French Doors

32" High Wall

Books/Cabinets

Living Room
13'-4" x 17'

Study
13'-4" x 15'

Foyer

Porch

WIDTH 59' 4"
DEPTH 72' 8"

9' Clg. Throughout
Unless Otherwise Noted

SECOND FLOOR

Bedroom 2
13'-4" x 12'-4"

Bath 2

Laundry

Up To Optional
3rd Floor

Deck

Bedroom 3
13'-4" x 12'-4"

French Doors

Master Bedroom
18'-4" x 15'-4"

Bath 3

Down

Linen

Marble Pedestal

Seat W/Storage

Down

Foyer Below

Dressing Table

Bedroom 4
13'-4" x 12'-8"

Bath

Gazebo Clg.
At Tub

Exercise Room
11'-4" x 8'

Linen

Seat

Seat

REAR VIEW

During the middle of the 19th Century, homes were inspired by Gothic Revival details. Later, turned posts and delicate spindles were added to the porches, along with eave brackets and ornate cornice trim. Referred to as Folk Victorians, these homes were built until the beginning of the 20th Century. As authentic as the exterior of this design is, the interior offers a wealth of luxury and elegance. Note formal and informal living areas, the centrally located kitchen, plentiful built-ins and ample storage. The secluded master suite with exercise room is beyond compare. Three additional bedrooms and a laundry room complete the second floor. A staircase leads to an optional 14' x 39' third floor area.

DESIGN	M9015
BEDROOMS	4
BATHROOMS	3½
FIRST FLOOR	1,948 Sq. Ft.
SECOND FLOOR	1,891 Sq. Ft.
TOTAL	3,839 Sq. Ft.
PRICE	A5

A raised front gable with decorative shingles and a porch with ornate posts and brackets recall the simple charm of the Folk Victorian cottages built throughout this country at the turn of the century. The family room focuses on a fireplace with flanking full-width windows. The country-style kitchen offers ample dining space with its large bay window. The master bedroom features a ten-foot ceiling, a private dressing area, and a walk-in closet. The laundry room is conveniently located close to bedrooms 2 and 3. Plans for a detached two-car garage are included.

Bedroom 3
11' x 12'-4"

Bedroom 2
10' x 10'

Kitchen
10' x 10'

Dining
10' x 10'

Util.

Bath 2

Family Room
14' x 19'-4"
10' Clg.

Bath

Master
Bedroom
11'-4" x 17'
10' Clg.

Porch

8' Clg. Throughout Unless Otherwise Noted

DESIGN M9032
BEDROOMS 3
BATHROOMS 2
SQUARE FOOTAGE 1,358
PRICE A1

WIDTH 43' 4"
DEPTH 40' 2"

LARRY W. GARNETT & ASSOCIATES, INC.

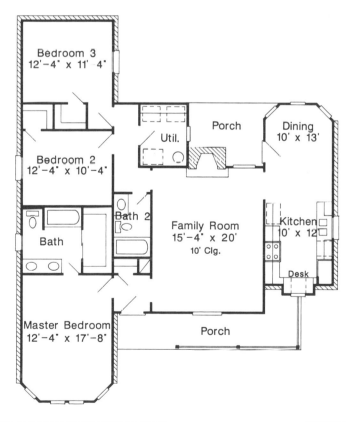

Bedroom 3
12'-4" x 11'-4"

Bedroom 2
12'-4" x 10'-4"

Porch

Util.

Dining
10' x 13'

Bath 2

Bath

Family Room
15'-4" x 20'
10' Clg.

Kitchen
10' x 12'

Desk

Master Bedroom
12'-4" x 17'-8"

Porch

8' Clg. Throughout Unless Otherwise Noted

While the roof line and porch details are reminiscent of a turn-of-the-century Farmhouse, the majority of the exterior is actually low-maintenance brick veneer. The family room, with its ten-foot ceiling, is a perfect area for relaxing or entertaining. A French door opens from the bay-windowed dining area to a covered porch. The efficiently designed kitchen has a built-in desk with a box window and lots of cabinet space. Located next to bedrooms 2 and 3, the laundry room has space for a freezer or additional storage. Plans are included for a detached two-car garage.

WIDTH 44' 8"
DEPTH 54' 2"

DESIGN M9033
BEDROOMS 3
BATHROOMS 2
SQUARE FOOTAGE 1,528
PRICE A1

This economical Farmhouse design offers a practical floor plan with some exciting surprises. The dining area is filled with natural light from a full-length bay window at the front of the house, while the kitchen area enjoys plenty of sun and light from the bay window over the sink. A nine-foot gambrel ceiling and fireplace add to the coziness of the family room. The private master bedroom has both a walk-in closet and a small linen closet. The laundry room is conveniently located next to bedrooms 2 and 3. Plans for a detached two-car garage are included.

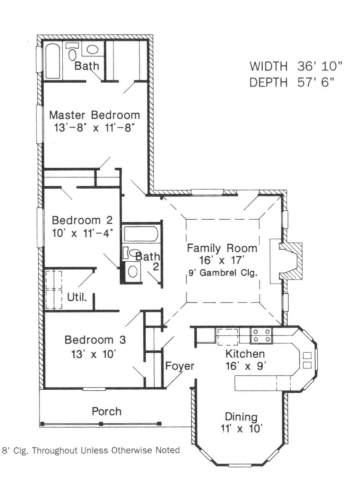

WIDTH 36' 10"
DEPTH 57' 6"

Bath

Master Bedroom
13'-8" x 11'-8"

Bedroom 2
10' x 11'-4"

Bath 2

Util.

Family Room
16' x 17'
9' Gambrel Clg.

Bedroom 3
13' x 10'

Foyer

Kitchen
16' x 9'

Porch

Dining
11' x 10'

8' Clg. Throughout Unless Otherwise Noted

DESIGN M9035
BEDROOMS 3
BATHROOMS 2
SQUARE FOOTAGE 1,341
PRICE A1

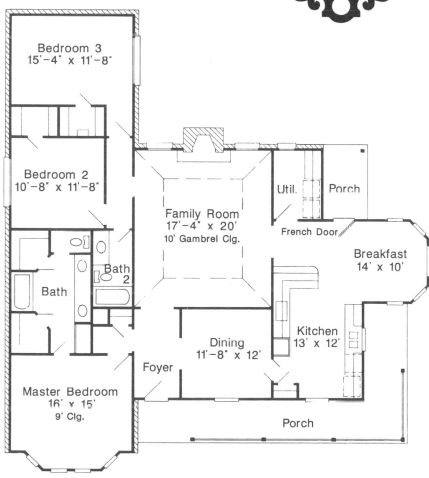

Bedroom 3
15'-4" x 11'-8"

Bedroom 2
10'-8" x 11'-8"

Family Room
17'-4" x 20'
10' Gambrel Clg.

Util.

Porch

French Door

Bath 2

Bath

Breakfast
14' x 10'

Kitchen
13' x 12'

Dining
11'-8" x 12'

Foyer

Master Bedroom
16' x 15'
9' Clg.

Porch

8' Clg. Throughout Unless Otherwise Noted

WIDTH 54' 2"
DEPTH 59' 6"

With its front bay window, wrap-around porch, and shutters, this home possesses both country charm and elegance. The foyer opens to a formal dining room, and a short hall that leads to the secluded master bedroom. The master bath features plenty of linen storage, along with His and Hers walk-in closets. The kitchen overlooks a large bay-windowed breakfast area and also offers a practical 42-inch-high eating bar. Full-length windows flanking a brick fireplace and a ten-foot gambrel ceiling are highlights of the family room. Bedrooms 2 and 3 each have large walk-in closets. Plans for a detached two-car garage are included.

DESIGN	M9039
BEDROOMS	3
BATHROOMS	2
SQUARE FOOTAGE	1,978
PRICE	A1

This practical and rather economical one-story Farmhouse design offers a wraparound front porch with ornate posts and railing. The living room not only features a ten-foot ceiling, but also offers expansive windows and a built-in bookcase. The kitchen, with its walk-in pantry, overlooks a large bay-windowed dining area. A cathedral ceiling enhances the master bedroom. His and Hers walk-in closets and a large linen closet are focal points of the master bath. Plans for a two-car detached garage are included.

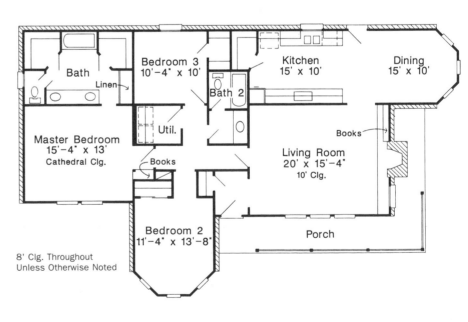

DESIGN M9038
BEDROOMS 3
BATHROOMS 2
SQUARE FOOTAGE 1,659
PRICE A1

WIDTH 63' 4"
DEPTH 37' 10"

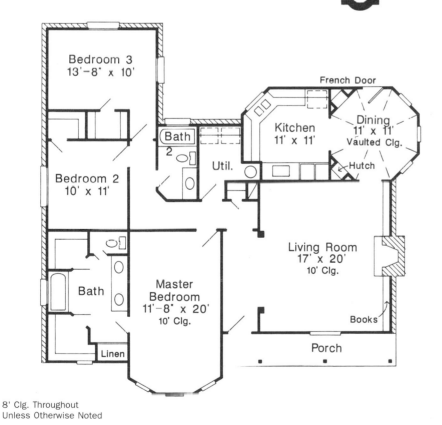

Bedroom 3
13'-8" x 10'

Bath
2

Kitchen
11' x 11'

French Door

Dining
11' x 11'
Vaulted Clg.

Hutch

Util.

Bedroom 2
10' x 11'

Living Room
17' x 20'
10' Clg.

Bath

Master
Bedroom
11'-8" x 20'
10' Clg.

Books

Linen

Porch

8' Clg. Throughout
Unless Otherwise Noted

WIDTH 48' 10"
DEPTH 46' 10"

Boasting an efficient floor plan with plenty of closet space, this Farmhouse is rather economical to build. The simple roof design and well-proportioned bay window and front porch, which are far less costly than many Farmhouse designs, allow extras such as the ten-foot ceilings in the master bedroom and the living room, and the unique "gazebo" vaulted ceiling in the dining area. Optional bookcases are located on each side of the fireplace. The laundry room is conveniently located near the bedrooms. The sides and part of the rear of the home are brick veneer, providing for much less maintenance and painting. Plans for a two-car detached garage are included with this design.

DESIGN M9007
BEDROOMS 3
BATHROOMS 2
SQUARE FOOTAGE 1,669
PRICE A1

Designed for casual living inside and out, this one-story Farmhouse is an ideal family home. The family room features a ten-foot ceiling and a corner fireplace. An enormous dining area can handle even the largest family dinners. The large rear porch is perfect for outdoor entertaining. The laundry room is conveniently located near the three bedrooms. His and Hers walk-in closets and twin lavatories are part of the luxurious master bath. Plans for a 24' x 24' detached garage are included with this design.

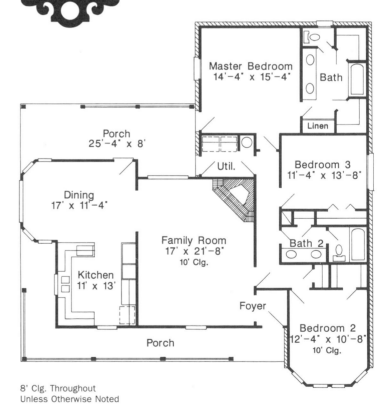

Master Bedroom
14'-4" x 15'-4"
Bath

Linen

Bedroom 3
11'-4" x 13'-8"

Porch
25'-4" x 8'

Util.

Dining
17' x 11'-4"

Bath 2

Family Room
17' x 21'-8"
10' Clg.

Kitchen
11' x 13'

Foyer

Bedroom 2
12'-4" x 10'-8"
10' Clg.

Porch

8' Clg. Throughout
Unless Otherwise Noted

DESIGN	M9006
BEDROOMS	3
BATHROOMS	2
SQUARE FOOTAGE	1,772
PRICE	A1

WIDTH 51' 2"
DEPTH 52' 10"

8' Clg. Throughout
Unless Otherwise Noted

FIRST FLOOR

With its brick-veneer exterior, dormer windows and wraparound porch, this home is a blend of the early 1900s Farmhouse and the Prairie Style. Corner box windows provide a cozy sitting area next to the fireplace in the family room. The efficient kitchen overlooks the breakfast area with its full-length windows. A French door opens to a large covered porch. Double doors open to the master bedroom with a ten-foot gambrel ceiling. The bath features mirrored closet doors and double lavatories. Upstairs, there are two bedrooms, each with dormer window alcoves and sloping ceilings. Plans for a two-car detached garage are included.

SECOND FLOOR

QUOTE ONE ®
Cost to build? See page 188 to order complete cost estimate to build this house in your area!

WIDTH 44'
DEPTH 45'

DESIGN M9074
BEDROOMS 3
BATHROOMS 2½
FIRST FLOOR 1,288 Sq. Ft.
SECOND FLOOR 495 Sq. Ft.
TOTAL 1,783 Sq. Ft.
PRICE A1

The timeless beauty and practicality of the wraparound veranda give this Farmhouse a casual, yet distinctive appearance. The efficiently designed kitchen opens to a light-filled breakfast area with full-length windows and a French door that leads to the veranda. The master suite offers His and Hers lavatories and a large walk-in closet. Upstairs, optional skylights provide plenty of natural light to the balcony. Two bedrooms share a bath that has separate bathing and dressing areas. Plans for a two-car detached garage are included.

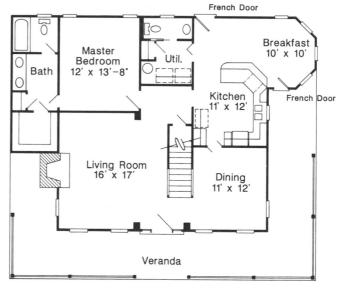

French Door

Master Bedroom 12' x 13'-8"

Util.

Breakfast 10' x 10'

French Door

Bath

Kitchen 11' x 12'

Living Room 16' x 17'

Dining 11' x 12'

Veranda

8' Clg. Throughout

FIRST FLOOR

Skylights

Bedroom 3 10'-8" x 13'

Bedroom 2 11' x 13'

Bath 2

← Slope →

← Slope →

Linen

SECOND FLOOR

DESIGN	M9003
BEDROOMS	3
BATHROOMS	2½
FIRST FLOOR	1,244 Sq. Ft.
SECOND FLOOR	551 Sq. Ft.
TOTAL	1,795 Sq. Ft.
PRICE	A4

WIDTH 46'
DEPTH 38' 8"

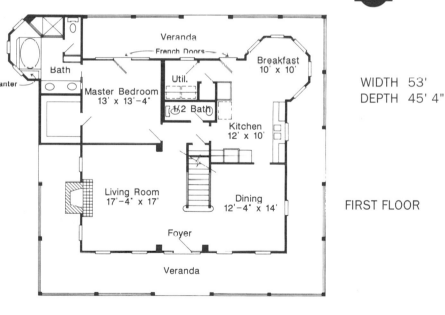

WIDTH 53'
DEPTH 45' 4"

FIRST FLOOR

9' Clg. Throughout

The wraparound veranda and simple, uncluttered lines give this home an unassuming elegance that is characteristic of its Farmhouse heritage. The kitchen overlooks an octagon-shaped breakfast room with full-length windows and a French door that opens to the rear veranda. An exceptional master bedroom provides plenty of closet space and an elegant bath. Located within an oversized bay window is a garden tub with adjacent planter and glass-enclosed shower. Upstairs, two bedrooms share a bath with separate dressing and bathing areas. The balcony sitting area is a perfect playroom or study area. Plans for a two-car garage are included.

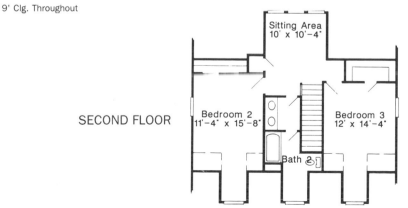

SECOND FLOOR

DESIGN M9001
BEDROOMS 3
BATHROOMS 2½
FIRST FLOOR 1,308 Sq. Ft.
SECOND FLOOR 751 Sq. Ft.
TOTAL 2,059 Sq. Ft.
PRICE A4

The symmetry and grace of the turn-of-the-century Farmhouse is captured in this design. The veranda provides plenty of shade for outdoor activities. Inside, the kitchen with center island work counter opens to the breakfast area with a full-length bay window. The master bedroom features a walk-in closet and abundant linen storage. A corner tub and glass-enclosed shower highlight the bath. An optional French door allows access to a swimming pool, or possibly a private spa. Upstairs, the balcony overlooks the living room below. Two bedrooms each have walk-in closets and private dressing areas. Plans for a detached two-car garage are included.

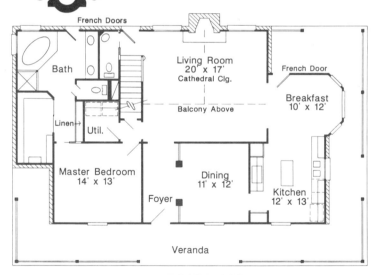

FIRST FLOOR

8' Clg. Throughout Unless Otherwise Noted

DESIGN	M9002
BEDROOMS	3
BATHROOMS	2½
FIRST FLOOR	1,504 Sq. Ft.
SECOND FLOOR	690 Sq. Ft.
TOTAL	2,194 Sq. Ft.
PRICE	A2

WIDTH 57' 4"
DEPTH 37' 8"

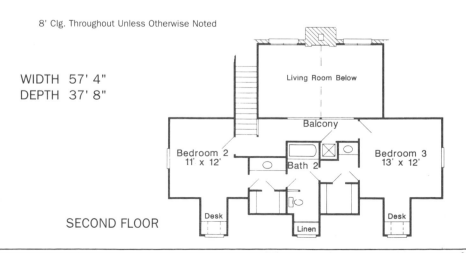

SECOND FLOOR

PRAIRIE-STYLE FARMHOUSE

Porch
French Door

Living Room
17' x 23'

Util.

Bath

Linen

Balcony Above

Breakfast
15' x 10'

Master Bedroom
15' x 17'

Dining
11' x 13'

Kitchen
11' x 16'

Foyer

32" High Wall

Veranda

8' Clg. Throughout

FIRST FLOOR

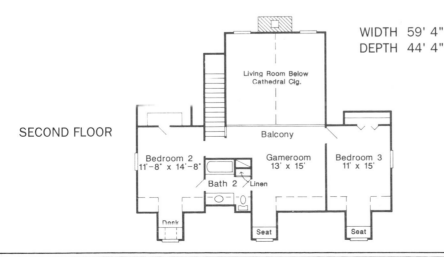

Living Room Below
Cathedral Clg.

SECOND FLOOR

Balcony

Bedroom 2
11'-8" x 14'-8"

Gameroom
13' x 15'

Bedroom 3
11' x 15'

Bath 2

Linen

Desk

Seat

Seat

WIDTH 59' 4"
DEPTH 44' 4"

The wraparound veranda of this Farmhouse design offers a shaded outdoor living area. Inside, an efficient floor plan provides plenty of open living areas. The foyer and formal dining room are separated by a 32-inch-high wall, while the kitchen opens directly to a spacious breakfast area. A small rear porch can be connected by a breezeway to the detached garage (plan included). The highlight of this home is the living room. A center fireplace with tall glass on each side soars to the top of the cathedral ceiling, while a balcony opens from the game room above. A French door opens to the rear porch. The master suite features His and Hers walk-in closets and abundant linen storage. Each upstairs bedroom offers a built-in desk or window seat.

DESIGN M9000
BEDROOMS 3
BATHROOMS 2½
FIRST FLOOR 1,669 Sq. Ft.
SECOND FLOOR 780 Sq. Ft.
TOTAL 2,449 Sq. Ft.
PRICE A5

This Farmhouse design will suit the needs of any large, active family. The foyer opens directly to the formal living room with an elegant fireplace. The family area offers a unique brick wall with built-in fireplace and a French door opening onto a covered porch. A well-planned kitchen overlooks a breakfast area with full-length windows that allow an uninterrupted view of the rear yard. The master bedroom, with third fireplace, has access to a private study. His and Hers walk-in closets, along with a garden tub and glass-enclosed shower, complete this secluded master suite. Upstairs, three bedrooms and two baths offer plenty of space and convenience for the children. A game room with an alcove provides a versatile family activity area.

Quote One®

Cost to build? See page 188 to order complete cost estimate to build this house in your area!

FIRST FLOOR

9' Clg. Throughout

SECOND FLOOR

DESIGN M9004
BEDROOMS 4
BATHROOMS 3½
FIRST FLOOR 2,166 Sq. Ft.
SECOND FLOOR 1,169 Sq. Ft.
TOTAL 3,335 Sq. Ft.
PRICE A5

WIDTH 74' 8"
DEPTH 71' 8

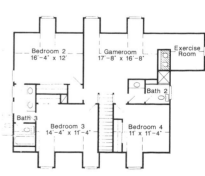

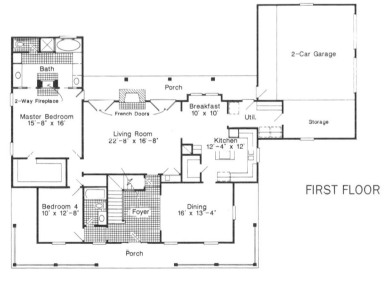

FIRST FLOOR

10' Clg. Throughout First Floor
Unless Otherwise Noted

Master Bedroom 15'-8" x 16'
Bath
2-Way Fireplace
Bedroom 4 10' x 12'-8"
Foyer
Living Room 22'-8" x 16'-8"
French Doors
Porch
Breakfast 10' x 10'
Util.
Kitchen 12'-4" x 12'
Dining 16' x 13'-4"
Porch
2-Car Garage
Storage

SECOND FLOOR

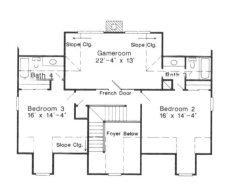

Gameroom 22'-4" x 13'
Slope Clg.
Bath 4
Bath
French Door
Bedroom 3 16' x 14'-4"
Bedroom 2 16' x 14'-4"
Foyer Below
Slope Clg.

9' Clg. Throughout Second Floor
Unless Otherwise Noted

WIDTH 79'
DEPTH 60' 6"

The wraparound front porch and dormer windows give this home a casual and comfortable appearance. The large living area features French doors on each side of an elegant fireplace, and a built-in wet bar. An island cooktop, along with a walk-in pantry, are part of the well-planned kitchen. The utility room, with extra work space, leads to an attached two-car garage and storage area. The master bedroom has generous closet space and a two-way fireplace opening into the master bath. Bedrooms 3 and 4 each have a private bath, while bedroom 2 shares access to a bath with the game room. Each upstairs bedroom has a sloped ceiling and a cozy alcove created by the dormer window.

DESIGN M9005
BEDROOMS 4
BATHROOMS 4
FIRST FLOOR 1,995 Sq. Ft.
SECOND FLOOR 1,077 Sq. Ft.
TOTAL 3,072 Sq. Ft.
PRICE A5

This home was inspired by the grand Farmhouses of the late 19th and early 20th Centuries, with their sprawling porches and Victorian-style gingerbread trim. The gallery leads from the elegant foyer to an enormous living and dining area. The spectacular kitchen opens directly to a windowed breakfast alcove and a light-filled sunroom, ideal for casual family living. Located off the kitchen is a walk-in pantry and a mudroom with additional storage. The first-floor master bedroom offers a secluded retreat. The bath area has His and Hers walk-in closets, a shower, and a garden tub with leaded-glass windows above. Upstairs, the two bedrooms each have private bathrooms and large walk-in closets. Includes plans for a detached two-car garage.

9' Clg. Throughout
Unless Otherwise Noted

FIRST FLOOR

DESIGN	M9075
BEDROOMS	3
BATHROOMS	3½
FIRST FLOOR	2,232 Sq. Ft.
SECOND FLOOR	808 Sq. Ft.
TOTAL	3,040 Sq. Ft.
PRICE	A5

WIDTH   75' 10"
DEPTH   46' 10"

SECOND FLOOR

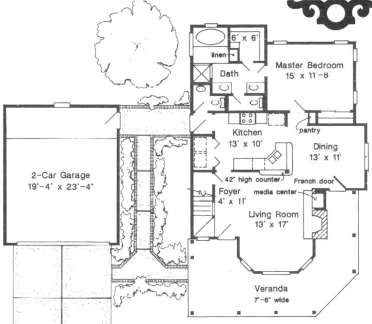

FIRST FLOOR

Labels within first floor plan:
6' x 6'
linen
Bath
Master Bedroom 15' x 11'-8"
pantry
Kitchen 13' x 10'
Dining 13' x 11'
42" high counter
French door
Foyer 4' x 11'
media center
Living Room 13' x 17'
Veranda 7'-6" wide

SECOND FLOOR

Labels within second floor plan:
3' x 8'
books
Bath
Bedroom 3 11' x 11'
Balcony
French door
Sunroom 8' x 7'
Bedroom 2 12'-8" x 11'-8"

2-Car Garage 19'-4" x 23'-4"

WIDTH 30' 10"
DEPTH 51'

This charming farmhouse, with its wide, wraparound veranda, supplies all the space needed for whittling and listening to cricket songs. Once inside, the charm continues with a foyer that opens to a bay-windowed living room with fireplace and media center. The thoughtfully designed kitchen furnishes a step-saving layout and a nearby formal dining room opens to the veranda through French doors. Privacy is paramount for the master suite carefully secluded to the rear of the main floor, but amenities abound. A large walk-in closet, dual vanities, separate tub and shower and a compartmented toilet add to a luxurious master bath. The second floor holds two secondary bedrooms, a full bath, a sunroom, a built-in bookcase and a large storage space.

DESIGN M8959
BEDROOMS 3
BATHROOMS 2½
FIRST FLOOR 1,051 Sq. Ft.
SECOND FLOOR 631 Sq. Ft.
TOTAL 1,682 Sq. Ft.
PRICE A3

LARRY W. GARNETT & ASSOCIATES, INC.

Larry W. Garnett & Associates, Inc. offers a complete and useful plan package as outlined below:

- Elevations of front, rear and sides
- Foundation plan (monolithic concrete slab)
- Detailed floor plan(s) with electrical and plumbing locations
- Cabinet, vanity and miscellaneous interior details
- Typical detail and section sheets
- Garage plan (A two-car garage plan is included at no extra charge with all plans designed for a detached garage. See illustration below.)
- Reversed plans are mirror-image with dimensions and lettering reading backwards.

Plans do not include specifications or heating and air conditioning layouts. Your local mechanical contractor will size and locate the proper equipment for your particular climatic conditions. Material lists are not included due to differences in construction practices and local availability of various materials.

Larry W. Garnett & Associates, Inc. makes no warranties, either expressed or implied, regarding plans. Purchasers should have plans reviewed by a licensed builder and architect before beginning construction. Modification may be necessary for compliance with local and state regulations and codes.

HOME PLAN PRICE SCHEDULE

#Sets	A1	A2	A3	A4	A5/A6
One	$395	445	495	545	595
Four	445	495	545	595	645
Eight	490	540	590	640	695
Repro	590	640	690	740	795

Additional single sets	$40
Mirror Reverse Surcharge	$50
Materials List	$50

(not available on all plans, please inquire when ordering)

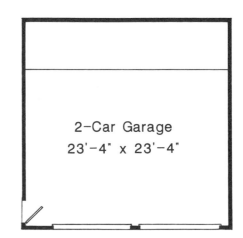

2-Car Garage
23'-4" x 23'-4"

TO ORDER BLUEPRINTS, TURN TO PAGE 187.

HOME PLANNERS

Home Planners is one of the longest-running and most successful home design firms in the United States. With over 2,500 designs in its portfolio, the company provides a wide range of styles, sizes and types of homes. It takes pride in producing one of the most complete and detailed blueprint packages available and offers a number of additional products, including a home-planning kit, construction details sets and materials lists for most of its designs.

With over 135 books and magazines to its credit, Home Planners has sold over 2½ million sets of blueprints since its inception in 1946. The company's plans are featured regularly in such popular magazines as *House Beautiful, Better Homes and Gardens, Practical Homeowner, Homeowner, Decorating/Remodeling* and others. Among the many books published by Home Planners are collections of exterior styles, design categories and portfolios. In addition to the plans, many of the publications provide special sections offering advice, building and design tips and helpful hints. Of particular note is *The Home Landscaper,* a bestselling guide to landscape design with 40 professionally designed plans the homeowner can create from blueprints.

Home Planners' portfolio of Victorian and Farmhouse design is a response to a growing demand for these styles. Rickard Bailey, President and Publisher of Home Planners, maintains, "Today, there is a return to traditionalism and pure styles. People want the look and feel of an older home with the amenities and comforts of modern floor planning. Elaborate master bedroom suites, cozy

country kitchens, libraries, media centers and great rooms are all a part of what makes a plan livable.

"Featured here are Victorian and Farmhouse designs created to meet the needs of today's sophisticated family. Ranging in size from 1,515 to 5,643 square feet, these plans represent some of the best examples of the genre. Included are 18 brand new, never-before-published plans, many with smaller square footages and all boasting features that enhance their appeal."

The featured Victorians are presented with all the architectural details that make this style so unique: sweeping wraparound verandas, Palladian windows, cornice adornments, spindlework and much more. Inside, they boast such sought-after amenities as pampering master bedroom suites, third-floor guest suites, studies, libraries, media rooms and exercise rooms.

The Farmhouses are a countrified collection of one- and two-story homes with rustic exterior detailing and interiors that have all the components of modern floor planning: gathering rooms, split-bedroom layouts, country kitchens and convenient service areas, as well as other contemporary comforts.

Concludes Bailey. "All of these plans have been created with the care and professional expertise that fifty years of experience in the home-planning business affords us. Though clearly visually appealing and true to their architectural past, these homes are designed to be built, lived in and enjoyed today and for years to come."

This delightful Victorian cottage features three floors of living potential and exterior details that perfectly complement the convenient plan inside. Note the central placement of the kitchen, near to the dining room and the family room. A lovely side porch is the ideal location for weekend relaxing. Two fireplaces keep things warm and cozy. Three second-floor bedrooms include a master suite with bay window and two family bedrooms, one with an alcove and walk-in closet. Use the third-floor studio as a study, office or playroom for the children.

QUOTE ONE™

Cost to build? See page 188 to order complete cost estimate to build this house in your area!

FIRST FLOOR

SECOND FLOOR

THIRD FLOOR

WIDTH 48'
DEPTH 46'

DESIGN	M3383
BEDROOMS	3
BATHROOMS	2½
FIRST FLOOR	995 Sq. Ft.
SECOND FLOOR	1,064 Sq. Ft.
THIRD FLOOR	425 Sq. Ft.
TOTAL	2,484 Sq. Ft.
PRICE	B3

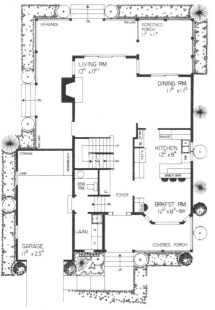

FIRST FLOOR

SECOND FLOOR

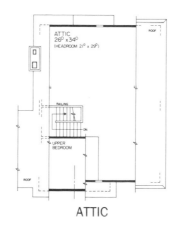

ATTIC

QUOTE ONE™

Cost to build? See page 188
to order complete cost estimate
to build this house in your area!

WIDTH 38'
DEPTH 52'

This house is but 38-feet wide. Its narrow width belies the tremendous amount of livability found inside. And, of course, the ubiquitous porch/veranda contributes mightily to style as well as livability. The efficient, U-shaped kitchen is flanked by the informal breakfast room and formal dining room. The rear living area is spacious and functions in an exciting manner with the outdoor areas. Upstairs, the master bedroom features a deluxe bath with a walk in closet, separate tub and shower, and a double vanity. Two additional bedrooms have extra large closets. Bonus recreational, hobby and storage space is offered in the basement and the attic.

California Engineered Plans and California Stock Plans are available for this home. Call 1-800-521-6797 for more information.

DESIGN	M2974
BEDROOMS	3
BATHROOMS	2½
FIRST FLOOR	911 Sq. Ft.
SECOND FLOOR	861 Sq. Ft.
TOTAL	1,772 Sq. Ft.
PRICE	B1

Covered porches front and rear are the first signal that this is a fine example of Folk Victorian styling. Complementing the exterior is a grand plan for family living. A formal living room and adjoining dining room create a lovely space for entertaining guests. The large family room with fireplace can be an everyday gathering room. Both formal and informal areas have access to outdoor spaces. Three bedrooms and a study or guest room with its own balcony occupy the second floor. The master suite features two lavatories, a window seat and three closets. Note the open staircase and convenient linen storage.

QUOTE ONE®

Cost to build? See page 188 to order complete cost estimate to build this house in your area!

FIRST FLOOR

SECOND FLOOR

DESIGN	M3385
BEDROOMS	3 or 4 (study)
BATHROOMS	2½
FIRST FLOOR	1,096 Sq. Ft.
SECOND FLOOR	900 Sq. Ft.
TOTAL	1,996 Sq. Ft.
PRICE	B3

WIDTH 56'
DEPTH 44'

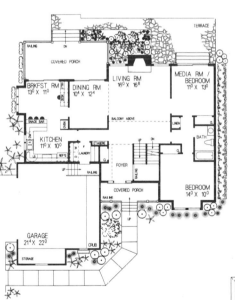

FIRST FLOOR

QUOTE ONE™

Cost to build? See page 188
to order complete cost estimate
to build this house in your area!

SECOND FLOOR

This two-story farmhouse will be a delight for those who spend much time working at home. The second floor offers the utmost in privacy, with a secluded master bedroom full of comforting features and a studio for more industrious pursuits. Downstairs is a very livable floor plan. A U-shaped kitchen with snack bar and breakfast area with bay window and desk are only the first of the eating areas, which extend to a formal dining room and a covered rear porch for dining al fresco. The two-story living room features a cozy fireplace. A versatile room to the back could serve as a media room or a third bedroom, sharing a full bath with the large front bedroom with bay window.

DESIGN	M3390
BEDROOMS	2 or 3
BATHROOMS	2
FIRST FLOOR	1,508 Sq. Ft.
SECOND FLOOR	760 Sq. Ft.
TOTAL	2,268 Sq. Ft.
PRICE	B3

WIDTH 52'

DEPTH 58' 6"

A stunning Victorian turret accents the facade of this compact three-story beauty, a promise of the exciting floor plan held inside. Downstairs rooms include a grand-sized living room/dining room combination that handles both formal and informal gatherings. The U-shaped kitchen has a snack-bar pass-through to the dining room. Just to the left of the entry foyer is a private study with wet bar. On the second floor are three bedrooms and two full baths. The master bedroom has a whirlpool spa and large walk-in closet. The third floor is a perfect location for a guest bedroom with private bath, dormer window and two closets. Be sure to notice the full-width covered porch stretching across the back of the house.

FIRST FLOOR

SECOND FLOOR

THIRD FLOOR

DESIGN	M3389
BEDROOMS	4
BATHROOMS	3½
FIRST FLOOR	1,161 Sq. Ft.
SECOND FLOOR	1,090 Sq. Ft.
THIRD FLOOR	488 Sq. Ft.
TOTAL	2,739 Sq. Ft.
PRICE	B3

QUOTE ONE™

Cost to build? See page 188
to order complete cost estimate
to build this house in your area!

WIDTH 40' 4"
DEPTH 68' 6"

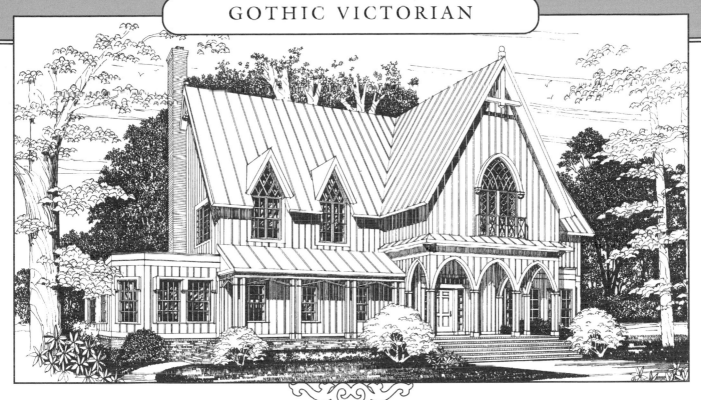

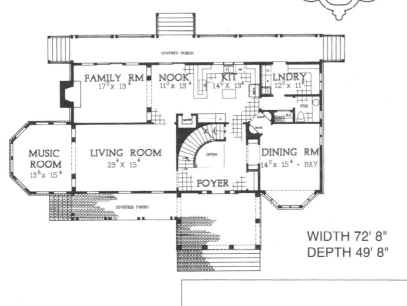

FAMILY RM 17⁰ x 13⁴   NOOK 11⁰ x 13⁴   KIT 14⁰ x 13⁴   LNDRY 12⁰ x 11⁸

MUSIC ROOM 13⁶ x 15⁴

LIVING ROOM 23⁴ x 15⁴

DINING RM 14⁰ x 15⁴ • BAY

FOYER

COVERED PORCH

WIDTH 72' 8"
DEPTH 49' 8"

MASTER BATH   WALK-IN CLOSET

BEDROOM 12⁸ x 11⁰   BEDROOM 12⁰ x 11⁸

WALK-IN CLOSET

MASTER BEDRM 23⁴ x 15⁴

VANITY

BEDROOM 14⁰ x 11⁸

HALL

LIBRARY/PLAY ROOM 18⁰ x 12⁶

This home's large foyer features a dramatic curving staircase to the second floor. The center entrance floor plan offers efficient and flexible traffic patterns. Formal living areas are located to the front of the plan; informal living areas are to the rear. The formal dining room is big and has a delightful bay window. The formal living room is spacious and functions through a pleasingly detailed columned archway with the cheerful music room. The rear kitchen is U-shaped with an island work surface and a walk-in pantry. The adjacent breakfast nook functions through sliding glass doors with the porch. Four bedrooms, three baths and a huge library/playroom grace the upstairs.

Quote One®

Cost to build? See page 188 to order complete cost estimate to build this house in your area!

DESIGN M3512
BEDROOMS 4
BATHROOMS 3½
FIRST FLOOR 1,983 Sq. Ft.
SECOND FLOOR 1,892 Sq. Ft.
TOTAL 3,875 Sq. Ft.
PRICE B4

A turreted facade, dormer window and fish-scale shingle details make this moderately sized Victorian stand out at a glance. Its well-designed floor plans make it even more attractive. Notice how guests as well as family are accommodated: powder room in the front foyer; gathering room with terrace access, fireplace and attached formal dining room; split-bedroom sleeping arrangements. The master suite contains His and Hers walk-in closets, a separate shower and whirl-pool tub and a delightful bay-windowed area. Upstairs there are three more bedrooms (one could serve as a study, one as a media room), a full bath and an open lounge area overlooking the gathering room. Notice the covered porches front and rear and long terrace area.

FIRST FLOOR

QUOTE ONE™

Cost to build? See page 188 to order complete cost estimate to build this house in your area!

SECOND FLOOR

DESIGN	M3393
BEDROOMS	3 or 4 (study or media room)
BATHROOMS	2½
FIRST FLOOR	1,449 Sq. Ft.
SECOND FLOOR	902 Sq. Ft.
TOTAL	2,351 Sq. Ft.
PRICE	B3

WIDTH 49'
DEPTH 54' 4"

QUOTE ONE™

Cost to build? See page 188
to order complete cost estimate
to build this house in your area!

FIRST FLOOR

SECOND FLOOR

WIDTH 57' 6"
DEPTH 46'

Classic Victorian styling comes to the forefront in this Queen Anne two-story. Complementary fishscale adorned pediments top the bayed tower to the left and garage to the right. Smaller versions are found at the dormer windows above a spindle-work porch. The interior boasts comfortable living quarters for the entire family. On opposite sides of the wide foyer are the formal dining and living rooms. To the rear is a country-style island kitchen with attached family room (don't miss the fireplace here). A small library shares a covered porch with this informal gathering area and also has its own fireplace. Three bedrooms on the second floor include a master suite with grand bath. The two family bathrooms share a full bath. Take special note of the service area conveniently attached to the two-car garage.

DESIGN	M3384
BEDROOMS	3
BATHROOMS	2½
FIRST FLOOR	1,399 Sq. Ft.
SECOND FLOOR	1,123 Sq. Ft.
TOTAL	2,522 Sq. Ft.
PRICE	B3

A simple but charming Queen Anne Victorian, this enchanting three-story home is our featured cover design. The exterior boasts delicately turned rails and decorated columns on its covered front porch. Just above is a small covered balcony off the master bedroom on the second floor. Inside is a family-oriented floor plan that includes a living room with fireplace and dining room that connects to the gourmet family kitchen via a wet bar. The adjoining family room contains another fireplace with a raised hearth complemented by flanking windows. The second floor holds two bedrooms, one a master suite with grand bath. A tucked-away guest suite on the third floor has its own private bath. Notice the unique gazebo projection off the covered porch to the rear of the plan.

Quote One™

Cost to build? See page 188 to order complete cost estimate to build this house in your area!

FIRST FLOOR

DESIGN	M3382
BEDROOMS	3
BATHROOMS	3½
FIRST FLOOR	1,366 Sq. Ft.
SECOND FLOOR	837 Sq. Ft.
THIRD FLOOR	363 Sq. Ft.
TOTAL	2,566 Sq. Ft.
PRICE	B3

SECOND FLOOR

WIDTH 50' 2"
DEPTH 69' 3"

THIRD FLOOR

RIGHT SIDE ELEVATION

REAR ELEVATION

One of the most popular features of the Victorian house has always been its covered porches. In addition to being an appealing design feature, covered porches have their practical side, too. They provide wonderful indoor/outdoor living relationships. Imagine sheltered outdoor living facilities for the various formal and informal living and dining areas of the plan. This home has a myriad of features to cater to the living requirements of the growing, active family. The modern kitchen features a snack bar and a desk. The luxurious master bath with His and Hers walk-in closets, a whirlpool tub and a double vanity will be greatly appreciated. Notice the built-in shelves in the bayed front bedroom.

California Engineered Plans and California Stock Plans are available for this home. Call 1-800-521-6797 for more information.

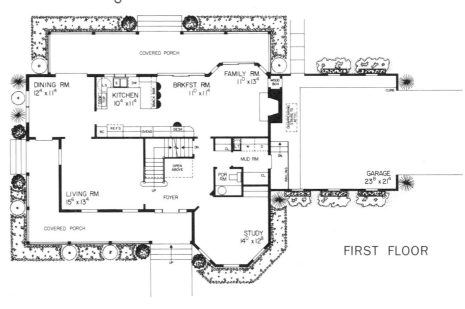

FIRST FLOOR

Quote One™

Cost to build? See page 188 to order complete cost estimate to build this house in your area!

SECOND FLOOR

DESIGN	M2973
BEDROOMS	4
BATHROOMS	2½
FIRST FLOOR	1,269 Sq. Ft.
SECOND FLOOR	1,227 Sq. Ft.
TOTAL	2,496 Sq. Ft.
PRICE	B2

WIDTH 70'
DEPTH 44' 5"

FIRST FLOOR

QUOTE ONE™

Cost to build? See page 188
to order complete cost estimate
to build this house in your area!

SECOND FLOOR

WIDTH 62' 7"
DEPTH 54'

Covered porches in the front and
back are a fine preview to the livable
nature of this Victorian. The expansive sunken family room features a
fireplace and access to the out-of-
doors. This plan includes both a
formal dining room with a bay and a
living room as well as a breakfast
room. The kitchen features a pass-
through and a large pantry. An
ample laundry room, garage with
storage area, and powder room round
out the first floor. The master
bedroom features an elegant bath
with a whirlpool tub, a separate
shower with a seat, and a double
vanity. Plenty of storage is available in
two closets. The second floor also
contains two additional bedrooms, a
study and a bath.

**California Engineered Plans and
California Stock Plans are available
for this home. Call 1-800-521-
6797 for more information.**

DESIGN	M3309
BEDROOMS	3
BATHROOMS	2½
FIRST FLOOR	1,375 Sq. Ft.
SECOND FLOOR	1,016 Sq. Ft.
TOTAL	2,391 Sq. Ft.
PRICE	B2

Though somewhat less elaborate than other Victorian types, the Folk Victorian is nevertheless an important and delightful interpretation as evidenced by this three-story example. From lovely covered front porch to classic rear veranda, it offers the finest in modern floor plans. The formal living areas are set off by a family room which connects the main house to the service areas. The laundry has room for not only a washer and dryer but also a freezer and sewing area. The second floor holds three bedrooms and two full baths. A sitting area in the master suite separates it from family bedrooms. On the third floor is a guest bedroom with gracious bath and large walk-in closet. Note the large storage area in the third-floor hall.

DESIGN M3394
BEDROOMS 4
BATHROOMS 3½
FIRST FLOOR 1,531 Sq. Ft.
SECOND FLOOR 1,307 Sq. Ft.
THIRD FLOOR 664 Sq. Ft.
TOTAL 3,502 Sq. Ft.
PRICE B4

FIRST FLOOR

SECOND FLOOR
WIDTH 70'
DEPTH 40'

THIRD FLOOR

Quote One™
Cost to build? See page 188 to order complete cost estimate to build this house in your area!

QUOTE ONE™

Cost to build? See page 188 to order complete cost estimate to build this house in your area!

FIRST FLOOR

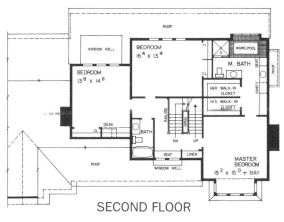

SECOND FLOOR

THIRD FLOOR

WIDTH 70'
DEPTH 44'

A testament to real Folk Victorian styling, this delightful home offers the best in thoughtful floor planning. From the covered front porch the home opens to a well-executed entry foyer. To the left is the casual family room with fireplace and proximity to the laundry and mud rooms. To the right is the formal living room with bay window and fireplace. This room connects to the formal dining area, also with bay window. The kitchen/breakfast room combination features sliding glass doors to the rear covered porch, an island cook top and large pantry. Second-floor bedrooms include a well-planned master suite and two family bedrooms served by a full bath. A guest room dominates the third floor and features its own private bath.

DESIGN M3388
BEDROOMS 4
BATHROOMS 3½+powder rm
FIRST FLOOR 1,517 Sq. Ft.
SECOND FLOOR 1,267 Sq. Ft.
THIRD FLOOR 480 Sq. Ft.
TOTAL 3,264 Sq. Ft.
PRICE B4

A quiet cottage—bringing to life the charm of a by-gone era, this 1½-story plan contains a commodious floor plan. The covered porch leads to a side-facing entry opening to a large, open foyer. To the front of the plan is the library with built-ins and a bay window seat. The kitchen and gathering room are to the rear of the plan. Notice the dining space in a windowed nook. Upstairs are two bedrooms and two full baths. The master suite has a walk-in closet and well-appointed bath.

Quote One®

Cost to build? See page 188 to order complete cost estimate to build this house in your area!

DESIGN M3522
BEDROOMS 2
BATHROOMS 2½
FIRST FLOOR 1,267 Sq. Ft.
SECOND FLOOR 833 Sq. Ft.
TOTAL 2,100 Sq. Ft.
PRICE B2

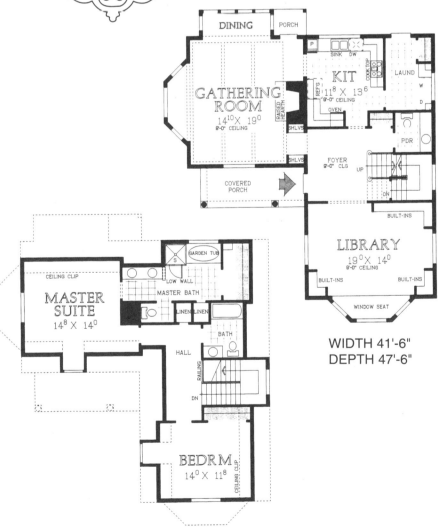

WIDTH 41'-6"
DEPTH 47'-6"

FIRST FLOOR

SECOND FLOOR

Quote One™

Cost to build? See page 188
to order complete cost estimate
to build this house in your area!

Classically styled, this charming design brings together the best in historical styling and modern floor planning. Special exterior features include three verandas, multi-paned windows and arch-topped windows. Inside, the first-floor plan boasts formal living and dining areas on either side of the entry foyer, a study that could double as a guest room with nearby full bath, a large family room with raised-hearth fireplace and snack bar pass-through, and a U-shaped kitchen with attached breakfast room. Two family bedrooms on the second floor share a full bath; the master bedroom has a thoughtfully appointed bath and large walk-in closet.

WIDTH 64'
DEPTH 51' 8"

DESIGN M3307
BEDROOMS 3 or 4 (study)
BATHROOMS 3
FIRST FLOOR 1,765 Sq. Ft.
SECOND FLOOR 1,105 Sq. Ft.
TOTAL 2,870 Sq. Ft.
PRICE B3

The stately proportions and exquisite Victorian detailing of this home are exciting indeed. Like so many Victorian houses, interesting roof lines set the character of this design. Observe the delightful mixture of gable roof, hip roof and dramatic turret. Horizontal siding, wood shingling, wide fascia, rake and corner boards make a strong statement. The delicate detailing of the windows, railings, cornices and front entry is most appealing to the eye. Inside is a very livable plan. The kitchen features a center island cooktop and shares a wide counter for casual dining with the adjoining family room. A bayed dining room with access to the rear porch is available for more formal occasions. Upstairs, each of the four bedrooms features a bay area and plenty of closet space. Don't miss the spacious master bath.

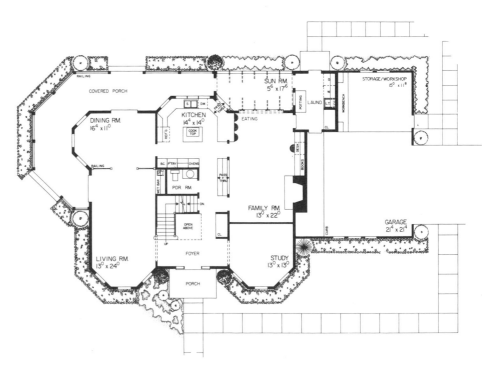

FIRST FLOOR

DESIGN	M2971
BEDROOMS	4
BATHROOMS	2½
FIRST FLOOR	1,766 Sq. Ft.
SECOND FLOOR	1,519 Sq. Ft.
TOTAL	3,285 Sq. Ft.
PRICE	B3

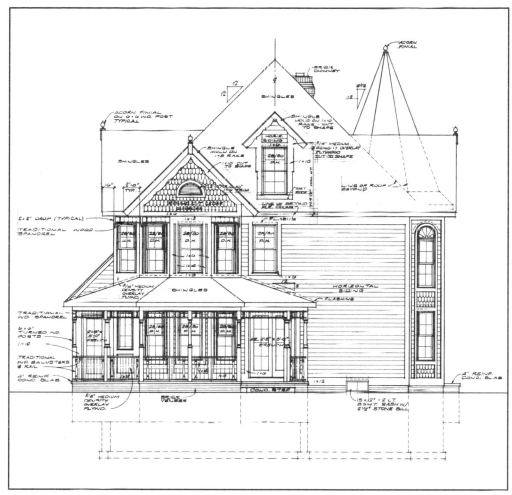

LEFT SIDE ELEVATION

WIDTH 77' 6"
DEPTH 44'

SECOND FLOOR

What can beat the charm of a tur-reted Victorian with covered porches to the front, side and rear? Projecting bays make their contribution to exterior styling and provide an extra measure of livability to the living, dining and family rooms, plus two of the bedrooms. The efficient kitchen, with its island cooking station, functions well with the dining and family rooms. A study provides a quiet first-floor haven for the family's less active pursuits. Upstairs, there are three big bedrooms and a fine master bath. A third floor provides a guest suite and huge bulk storage area (make it a cedar closet if you wish). This house has a basement for the development of further recreational and storage facilities. Note the two fireplaces, large laundry and attached two-car garage.

DESIGN M2969
BEDROOMS 4
BATHROOMS 3½
FIRST FLOOR 1,618 Sq. Ft.
SECOND FLOOR 1,315 Sq. Ft.
THIRD FLOOR 477 Sq. Ft.
TOTAL 3,410 Sq. Ft.
PRICE B3

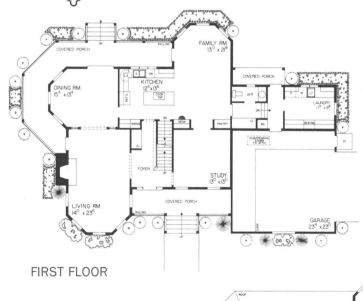

FIRST FLOOR

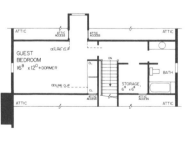

THIRD FLOOR

WIDTH 71' 8"
DEPTH 48' 4"

SECOND FLOOR

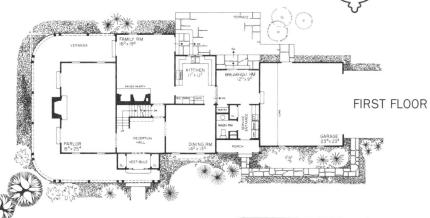

FIRST FLOOR

SECOND FLOOR

THIRD FLOOR

WIDTH 88'
DEPTH 42'

Reminiscent of the Gothic Victorian style of the mid-19th Century, this delightfully detailed, three-story house has a wraparound veranda for summertime relaxing. A grand reception hall welcomes visitors and displays an elegant staircase. The parlor and family room, each with a fireplace, provide excellent formal and informal living facilities. The well-planned kitchen is only a couple of steps from the dining and breakfast rooms. Access to the rear terrace is provided through the family room or the breakfast room. The second floor has four bedrooms and two baths plus a sewing room or study. The third floor houses an additional bedroom or studio with a half bath, as well as a playroom.

DESIGN	M2645
BEDROOMS	4
BATHROOMS	2½+powder rm
FIRST FLOOR	1,600 Sq. Ft.
SECOND FLOOR	1,095 Sq. Ft.
THIRD FLOOR	911 Sq. Ft.
TOTAL	3,606 Sq. Ft.
PRICE	B3

This home is a lovely example of classic Queen Anne architecture with two turrets, and pediments over the entry and three dormer-style window areas. Its floor plan offers over 5,000 square feet of living potential in three floors. On the first floor are the activity areas: a gathering room with fireplace, a study with an octagonal window area, a formal dining room and a kitchen with attached breakfast room. Bedrooms on the second floor include three family bedrooms and a grand master suite with sitting area, dressing room and master bath. A large attic storage area is found over the garage. On the third floor are a guest room with private bath and sitting area, and a game room with attached library.

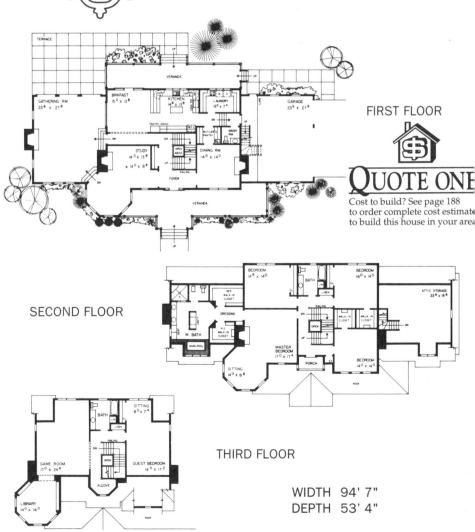

FIRST FLOOR

QUOTE ONE

Cost to build? See page 188 to order complete cost estimate to build this house in your area

SECOND FLOOR

THIRD FLOOR

WIDTH 94' 7"
DEPTH 53' 4"

DESIGN	M3395
BEDROOMS	5
BATHROOMS	3½
FIRST FLOOR	2,248 Sq. Ft.
SECOND FLOOR	2,020 Sq. Ft.
THIRD FLOOR	1,117 Sq. Ft.
TOTAL	5,385 Sq. Ft.
PRICE	B5

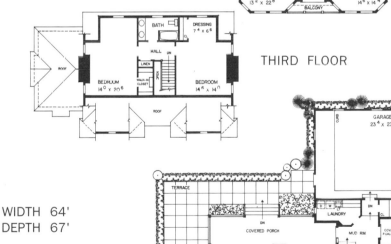

QUOTE ONE®

Cost to build? See page 188
to order complete cost estimate
to build this house in your area!

SECOND FLOOR

THIRD FLOOR

WIDTH 64'
DEPTH 67'

FIRST FLOOR

This beautiful Folk Victorian has all the properties of others in its class but measures them out in proportions that make it seem estate-like. The interior amenities are found on a corresponding scale as well. Living areas include a formal Victorian parlor, a private study and large gathering room. The formal dining room has its more casual counterpart in a bay-windowed breakfast room. Both are near the well-appointed kitchen. Five bedrooms serve family and guest needs handily. Three bedrooms on the second floor include a luxurious master suite. For outdoor entertaining or simply weekend relaxing, there is a covered rear porch leading to a terrace.

DESIGN	M3386
BEDROOMS	5
BATHROOMS	3½
FIRST FLOOR	1,683 Sq. Ft.
SECOND FLOOR	1,388 Sq. Ft.
THIRD FLOOR	808 Sq. Ft.
TOTAL	3,879 Sq. Ft.
PRICE	B5

Named for the architect, Henry Hobson Richardson, the Richardson Romanesque is known for being ample in size and substantial in appearance. This three-story example is indicative of the style's best characteristics. Complementary arched turrets on the outside give way to a wonderfully convenient floor plan. Formal and informal living areas occupy the first floor in a living room, dining room, family room and grand country kitchen. Upstairs are two family bedrooms and a lavish master suite with sitting area. The third floor contains another bedroom and private bath that could serve guests or live-ins quite well. Full-width verandas, front and back, provide indoor/outdoor living relationships and add just the right Victorian touch.

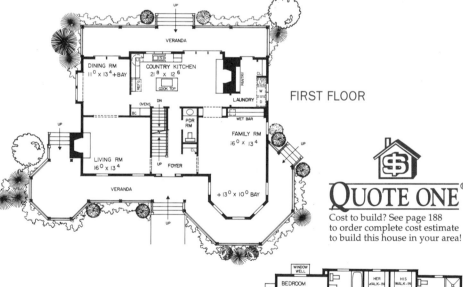

FIRST FLOOR

SECOND FLOOR

QUOTE ONE®

Cost to build? See page 188 to order complete cost estimate to build this house in your area!

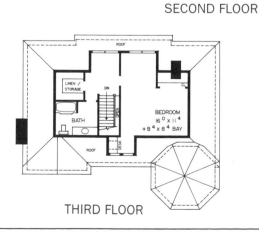

THIRD FLOOR

DESIGN	M3392
BEDROOMS	4
BATHROOMS	3½
FIRST FLOOR	1,405 Sq. Ft.
SECOND FLOOR	1,430 Sq. Ft.
THIRD FLOOR	624 Sq. Ft.
TOTAL	3,459 Sq. Ft.
PRICE	B4

WIDTH 62' 4"
DEPTH 51' 4"

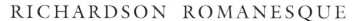

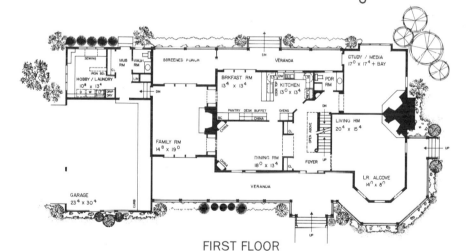

FIRST FLOOR

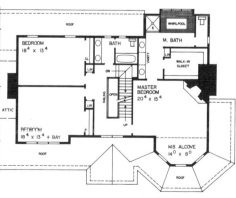

SECOND FLOOR

THIRD FLOOR

WIDTH 100'
DEPTH 48'

Another design that borrows from the forceful style of Henry Hobson Richardson; this home features a rounded turret top and rounded arches on the turret's windows. The interior allows plenty of room for busy lifestyles. Besides formal living and dining rooms and a casual family gathering room, there is a study with corner fireplace that also serves as a media room. Three bedrooms are found on the second floor along with two full baths. The third floor contains another bedroom with full bath and small alcove. Wide verandas both front and rear and a screened porch just off the family room allow good indoor/outdoor living relationships. Notice the large hobby/ laundry area connecting the house to the garage.

DESIGN M3387
BEDROOMS 4
BATHROOMS 3½+powder rm
FIRST FLOOR 2,393 Sq. Ft.
SECOND FLOOR 1,703 Sq. Ft.
THIRD FLOOR 716 Sq. Ft.
TOTAL 4,812 Sq. Ft.
PRICE B5

This charming Victorian features a covered outdoor living area on all four sides! It even ends as a screened porch with a sun deck above. This interesting plan offers three floors of livability. And what livability it is! Fireplaces can be found in the living room, family room and master suite. Plenty of formal and informal living facilities to go along with the potential of five bedrooms. The master suite is just that—a full suite. It is adjacent to an interesting sitting room and sports a sun deck and excellent bath/personal care facilities. The third floor will make a wonderful haven for the family's student members.

California Engineered Plans and California Stock Plans are available for this home. Call 1-800-521-6797 for more information.

FIRST FLOOR

DESIGN	M2970
BEDROOMS	4 or 5 (study)
BATHROOMS	3½
FIRST FLOOR	1,538 Sq. Ft.
SECOND FLOOR	1,526 Sq. Ft.
THIRD FLOOR	658 Sq. Ft.
TOTAL	3,722 Sq. Ft.
PRICE	B4

WIDTH 67'
DEPTH 66'

Quote One®

Cost to build? See page 188 to order complete cost estimate to build this house in your area!

LEFT SIDE ELEVATION

SECOND FLOOR

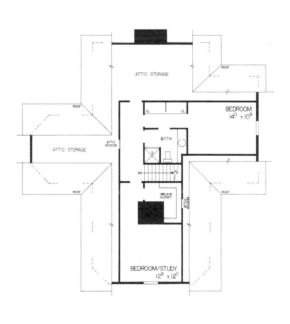

THIRD FLOOR

FIRST FLOOR

Victorian Style is displayed in exquisite proportions in this three-bedroom, four-bath home. From verandas, both front and rear, to the stately turrets and impressive chimney stack, this home is a beauty. Inside is a superb floor plan with many thoughtful amenities. The large living room and two-story family room both have fireplaces. To the front, there is a cozy study for private time. A gourmet kitchen with built-ins has a pass-through counter to the breakfast room. The bayed formal dining room has access to both the front and rear verandas. The master suite on the second floor includes many special features: whirlpool spa, separate shower, His and Hers walk-in closets, a private vanity, large exercise room, and a fireplace. There are two more bedrooms, each with a full bath, on the second floor.

SECOND FLOOR

QUOTE ONE™

Cost to build? See page 188 to order complete cost estimate to build this house in your area!

DESIGN	M3304
BEDROOMS	3
BATHROOMS	4
FIRST FLOOR	2,102 Sq. Ft.
SECOND FLOOR	1,971 Sq. Ft.
TOTAL	4,073 Sq. Ft.
PRICE	B5

WIDTH 87'
DEPTH 58' 6"

QUEEN ANNE

FIRST FLOOR

Quote One™

Cost to build? See page 188
to order complete cost estimate
to build this house in your area!

SECOND FLOOR

THIRD FLOOR

WIDTH 90' 6"
DEPTH 60'

Uniquely shaped rooms and a cache of amenities highlight this three-story beauty. The large sunken family room features a fireplace, wet bar and built-in seat. A liberal amount of work space is available in the kitchen, the breakfast room with built-in desk, and the laundry. Notice the abundance of storage space and the butler's pantry. A four-car garage easily holds the family fleet. The second floor has two family bedrooms and a full bath plus a master suite with His and Hers closets, multiple vanities and a whirlpool bath. An exercise room on the third floor has its own sauna and bath, while the large guest room on this floor is complemented by a charming alcove and another full bath.

DESIGN M3308
BEDROOMS 4
BATHROOMS 4½+powder rm
FIRST FLOOR 2,515 Sq. Ft.
SECOND FLOOR 1,708 Sq. Ft.
THIRD FLOOR 1,001 Sq. Ft.
TOTAL 5,224 Sq. Ft.
PRICE B5

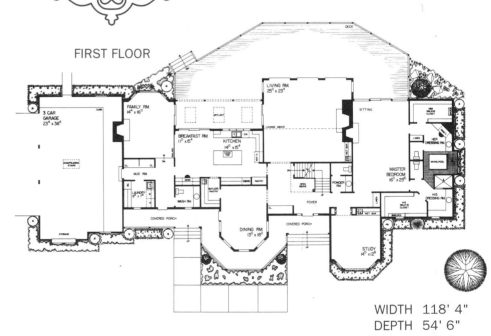

FIRST FLOOR

This enchanting manor displays architectural elements typical of the Victorian Style: asymmetrical facade, decorative shingles and gables, and a covered porch. The two-story living room with fireplace and wet bar opens to the glass-enclosed rear porch with skylights. A spacious kitchen is filled with amenities, including a butler's pantry connecting to the dining room. The master suite, adjacent to the study, opens to the rear deck. A cozy fireplace keeps the room warm on chilly evenings. The second floor opens to a large lounge with built-in cabinets and bookshelves. Three bedrooms and two full baths complete the second-floor livability. The three-car garage contains disappearing stairs to an attic storage area.

WIDTH 118' 4"
DEPTH 54' 6"

SECOND FLOOR

DESIGN	M2954
BEDROOMS	4
BATHROOMS	3½+powder rm
FIRST FLOOR	3,079 Sq. Ft.
SECOND FLOOR	1,461 Sq. Ft.
TOTAL	4,540 Sq. Ft.
PRICE	B5

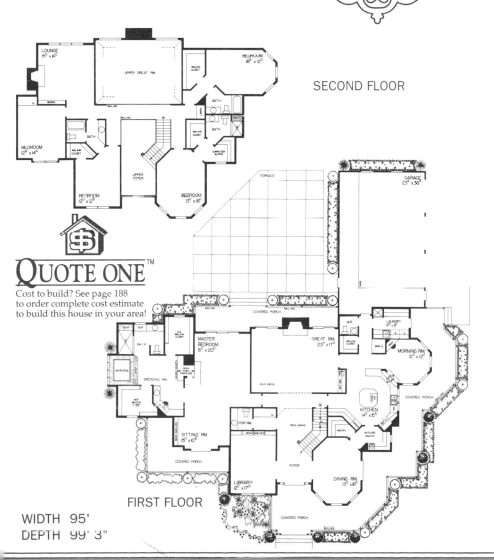

SECOND FLOOR

Quote One™

Cost to build? See page 188 to order complete cost estimate to build this house in your area!

FIRST FLOOR

WIDTH 95'
DEPTH 99' 3"

A magnificent, finely wrought covered porch wraps around this impressive Victorian estate home. To the left of the foyer is a bookshelf-lined library and to the right is a dramatic, octagonal-shaped dining room. The island cooktop completes a convenient work triangle in the kitchen, and a pass-through connects this room with the Victorian-style morning room. A luxurious master suite is located on the first floor and opens to the rear covered porch. A through-fireplace warms the bed-room, sitting room and dressing room, which includes His and Hers walk-in closets. Four uniquely designed bedrooms, three full baths, and a restful lounge with fireplace are located on the second floor.

California Engineered Plans and California Stock Plans are available for this home. Call 1-800-521-6797 for more information.

DESIGN	M2953
BEDROOMS	5
BATHROOMS	4 ½+powder rm
FIRST FLOOR	2,995 Sq. Ft.
SECOND FLOOR	1,831 Sq. Ft.
TOTAL	4,826 Sq. Ft.
PRICE	B5

This Victorian farmhouse seems to reach right out and greet you. The octagonal entry hall is balanced by two bay windows—one belonging to the master bedroom, the other to the formal dining room. Inside, Colonial columns and pilasters provide a charming entrance to a two-story family/great room enhanced by a fireplace and three sets of French doors. An arched opening leads to the L-shaped country kitchen highlighted by a bay-windowed eating area with a window seat. The spacious first-floor master suite is complemented by French doors opening onto the porch and a wealth of closet space. The second floor holds two secondary bedrooms and a full bath. Plans for an optional indoor swimming pool/spa and detached garage are included.

QUOTE ONE®

Cost to build? See page 188 to order complete cost estimate to build this house in your area!

WIDTH 50'
DEPTH 55'-3"

DESIGN	M3620
BEDROOMS	3
BATHROOMS	2½
FIRST FLOOR	1,295 Sq. Ft.
SECOND FLOOR	600 Sq. Ft.
TOTAL	1,895 Sq. Ft.
PRICE	B2

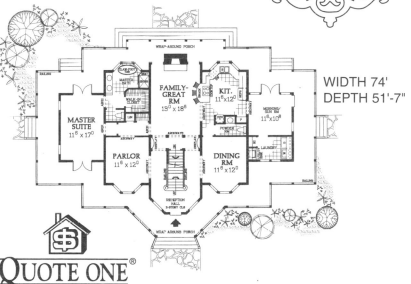

WIDTH 74'
DEPTH 51'-7"

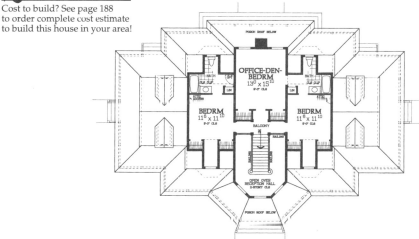

QUOTE ONE®

Cost to build? See page 188
to order complete cost estimate
to build this house in your area!

Delightfully proportioned and perfectly symmetrical, this Victorian farmhouse has lots of curb appeal. The wraparound porch offers rustic columns and railings and broad steps present easy access to the front, rear and side yards. Archways, display niches and columns catch the eye on the way to the large family/ great room with a fireplace. Flanking the reception hall are the formal parlor and the dining room. The left wing of the plan is devoted to the master suite. French doors provide direct access to the front and rear porches. The master bath is compartmented and has a bay with a claw-foot tub, twin lavatories, a walk-in closet and a stall shower with a seat. Upstairs, a perfectly symmetrical layout presents a big office/den (or make it a bedroom) flanked by two bedrooms, each with a full bath.

DESIGN	M3621
BEDROOMS	4
BATHROOMS	3½
FIRST FLOOR	1,752 Sq. Ft.
SECOND FLOOR	906 Sq. Ft.
TOTAL	2,658 Sq. Ft.
PRICE	B3

This Neo-Victorian design with its many gables offers plenty of roomy comfort. The first floor includes a living room with fireplace and bay window, family room with fireplace, formal dining room, modern kitchen with snack bar and breakfast room, as well as a large foyer with a convenient powder room. Note the second staircase in the utility room. The second floor includes a master bedroom suite with three closets, a dressing room and a separate tub and shower; three other large bedrooms; and a large studio that could also double as a room for hobbies or storage. The third floor includes a guest bedroom with bath and an upper lounge.

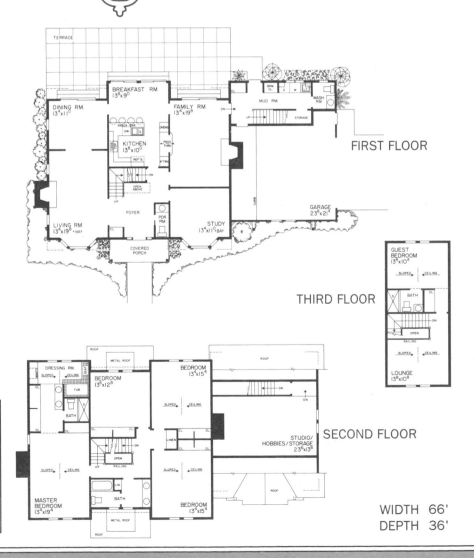

FIRST FLOOR

THIRD FLOOR

SECOND FLOOR

DESIGN	M2874
BEDROOMS	5
BATHROOMS	3½+powder rm
FIRST FLOOR	1,661 Sq. Ft.
SECOND FLOOR	1,808 Sq. Ft.
THIRD FLOOR	436 Sq. Ft.
TOTAL	3,905 Sq. Ft.
PRICE	B4

WIDTH 66'
DEPTH 36'

FIRST FLOOR

Detailed with gingerbread woodwork and a handsome double-width chimney, this two-story Neo-Victorian is breathtaking. Enter this home by way of the large, tiled receiving hall. The formal living room is spacious, with a fireplace and access to the covered porch. The dining room has a delightful bay window and is convenient to the kitchen for entertaining. The library is tucked between these two formal areas. The informal family room, with its L-shaped snack bar, will be a great place for family activities. Exploring the second floor reveals two bedrooms with two full bathrooms, and a third family bedroom nearby. The gracious master suite features His and Hers baths and a host of other features.

SECOND FLOOR

WIDTH 81'
DEPTH 52' 8"

DESIGN	M2829
BEDROOMS	5
BATHROOMS	4
FIRST FLOOR	2,044 Sq. Ft.
SECOND FLOOR	1,962 Sq. Ft.
TOTAL	4,006 Sq. Ft.
PRICE	B4

This country home creates an atmosphere as warm and comfortable as Grandma's feather bed. To the rear of the foyer, a two-story great room with a fireplace captures your immediate attention. An adjacent nook provides access to the covered porch via French doors, and combines with a snack bar and U-shaped kitchen for efficiency. The left wing contains a first-floor master suite designed for maximum privacy. French doors in the master bedroom extend an invitation to enjoy soft, summer breezes while the pampering master bath provides its own soothing relaxation. The second floor contains two family bedrooms that share a full bath.

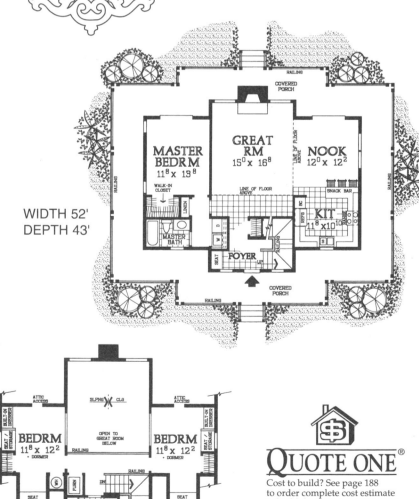

WIDTH 52'
DEPTH 43'

DESIGN M3673
BEDROOMS 3
BATHROOMS 2
FIRST FLOOR 1,086 Sq. Ft.
SECOND FLOOR 554 Sq. Ft.
TOTAL 1,640 Sq. Ft.
PRICE B2

Quote One®

Cost to build? See page 188
to order complete cost estimate
to build this house in your area!

WIDTH 52'
DEPTH 49'

Shingles, shutters and a flower box enjoyed from the kitchen window dress up this winsome country composition. From the covered front porch to the covered rear patio, amenities abound. Inside, to the right of the foyer, a formal dining room is defined by columns. Here, easy access is provided to the efficient U-shaped kitchen which features a convenient pantry. A large great room is enhanced by a warming fireplace and access to the rear patio. Two family bedrooms and a bath-and-a-half complete the first floor. Upstairs, the master suite reigns supreme. The deluxe master bath is highlighted by a relaxing garden tub, a separate shower, a dual-bowl vanity and an oversized walk-in closet.

QUOTE ONE®

Cost to build? See page 188
to order complete cost estimate
to build this house in your area!

DESIGN	M3678
BEDROOMS	3
BATHROOMS	2½
FIRST FLOOR	1,393 Sq. Ft.
SECOND FLOOR	487 Sq. Ft.
TOTAL	1,880 Sq. Ft.
PRICE	B2

This masterfully affordable Farm-house manages to include all the basics—then add a little more. Note the wraparound covered porch, large family room with raised-hearth fireplace and wet bar, spacious kitchen with island cooktop, formal dining room and rear terrace. Up-stairs, the plan is as flexible as they come: three or four bedrooms (the fourth could easily be a study or playroom) and plenty of unfinished attic just waiting to be transformed into living space. This area would make a fine sewing room, home office or children's playroom. Special amenities make this home a standout from others in its class. Note the many built-ins, the sliding glass doors to the terrace and the wealth of closets and storage space.

FIRST FLOOR

SECOND FLOOR

ATTIC

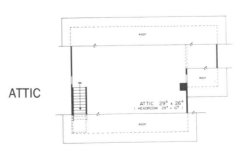

WIDTH 59' 8"
DEPTH 56'

DESIGN	M2945
BEDROOMS	3 or 4 (study)
BATHROOMS	2½
FIRST FLOOR	1,644 Sq. Ft.
SECOND FLOOR	971 Sq. Ft.
TOTAL	2,615 Sq. Ft.
PRICE	B2

FIRST FLOOR

SECOND FLOOR

WIDTH 62'
DEPTH 42'

The charm of early America is exemplified in this delightful Farmhouse design. Beyond its country-style facade lies a modern vital floor plan. The entry foyer opens the way to formal gatherings. To the left is the parlor with fireplace and formal dining room with bay window. To the right is the comfortable family room with raised-hearth through-fireplace to the casual dining area. A U-shaped kitchen is handy for both living areas. Upstairs are three bedrooms; the master is lavishly appointed with three closets, a dressing room and double vanities. Note the large storage area accessed through the closet. Two family bedrooms share a full bath.

DESIGN	M2681
BEDROOMS	3
BATHROOMS	2½
FIRST FLOOR	1,350 Sq. Ft.
SECOND FLOOR	1,224 Sq. Ft.
TOTAL	2,574 Sq. Ft.
PRICE	B2

Here's a traditional Farmhouse design that's made for down-home hospitality. The star attractions are the large covered porch and terrace. Inside, though, the design is truly a hard worker: separate living and family rooms, each with its own fireplace; formal dining room; large kitchen and breakfast area with bay window; separate study; workshop with plenty of room to maneuver; mud room; and four bedrooms upstairs. The master suite has an amenity-laden bath with window seat, vanity area and His and Hers walk-in closets. Don't miss the other extras throughout the home: curio niches, built-in bookshelves, entry powder room, kitchen pass-through, pantry, planning desk and workbench.

SECOND FLOOR

QUOTE ONE™

Cost to build? See page 188 to order complete cost estimate to build this house in your area!

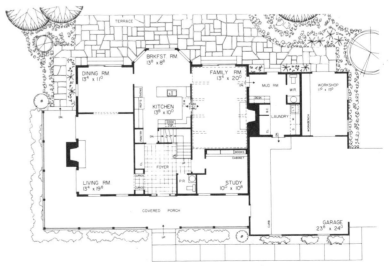

FIRST FLOOR

DESIGN	M2946
BEDROOMS	4
BATHROOMS	2½+powder rm
FIRST FLOOR	1,581 Sq. Ft.
SECOND FLOOR	1,344 Sq. Ft.
TOTAL	2,925 Sq. Ft.
PRICE	B3

WIDTH 74'
DEPTH 46'

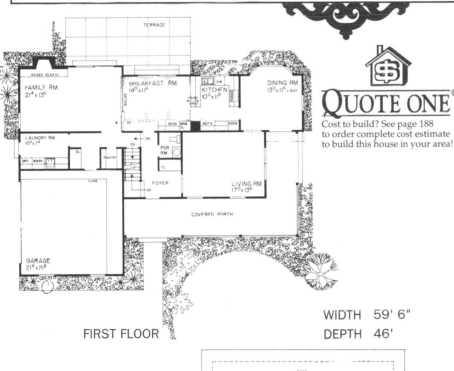

FIRST FLOOR

SECOND FLOOR

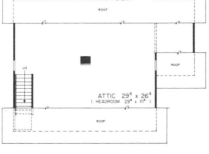

ATTIC

Quote ONE®

Cost to build? See page 188
to order complete cost estimate
to build this house in your area!

WIDTH 59' 6"
DEPTH 46'

This Classic Farmhouse has all the most up-to-date features expected in a new home. Beginning with the formal areas, this design offers something for the whole family. There is the quiet corner living room which has an opening to the sizable dining room, conveniently located, with the efficient U-shaped kitchen just a step away. The kitchen features many built-ins and a pass-through to the beamed-ceiling breakfast room. Sliding glass doors to the terrace are fine attractions in both the sunken family room and breakfast room. Upstairs are four bedrooms (or make one a study) and two baths, including the master suite with dressing area and double vanity.

California Engineered Plans and California Stock Plans are available for this home. Call 1-800-521-6797 for more information.

DESIGN	M2774
BEDROOMS	3 or 4 (study)
BATHROOMS	2½
FIRST FLOOR	1,366 Sq. Ft.
SECOND FLOOR	969 Sq. Ft.
TOTAL	2,335 Sq. Ft.
PRICE	B2

This two-story Farmhouse faithfully recalls the 18th-Century homestead of Secretary of Foreign Affairs John Jay. However, its floor plan can easily keep pace with the most modern of residences. The large entry foyer features a grand double staircase to the second floor. To the left is an extravagant country kitchen with fireplace and clutter room beyond. The living room with music alcove and fireplace are to the right; the formal dining room connects this room with the kitchen. A quiet library is tucked away in a far wing of the house; it enjoys a third fireplace. Upstairs, there are three comfortable bedrooms. Notice that covered porches grace both the front and rear of this grand home.

California Engineered Plans and California Stock Plans are available for this home. Call 1-800-521-6797 for more information.

DESIGN M2694
BEDROOMS 3
BATHROOMS 2½+powder rm
FIRST FLOOR 2,026 Sq. Ft.
SECOND FLOOR 1,386 Sq. Ft.
TOTAL 3,412 Sq. Ft.
PRICE B3

Quote One™

Cost to build? See page 188 to order complete cost estimate to build this house in your area!

FIRST FLOOR

SECOND FLOOR

WIDTH 84'
DEPTH 65' 8"

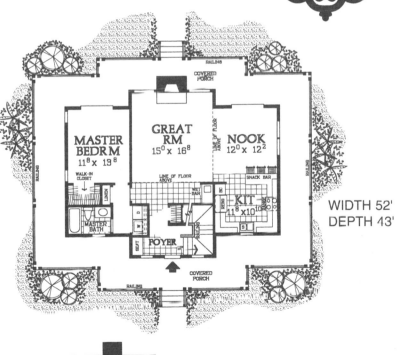

WIDTH 52'
DEPTH 43'

A wraparound porch, a welcoming entrance, and a thoughtful floor plan make this house a pleasure to come home to. The foyer, featuring a built-in seat with shoe storage, opens onto a large living area. Here, in the great room, a fireplace framed by unique windows provides focal interest. The adjacent nook and efficient kitchen combine with the great room to create a spacious area for formal and informal gatherings. The relaxing first-floor master suite is destined to become a favorite getaway. Skylights enhance the second floor and brighten a bridge that connects two family bedrooms to a full bath.

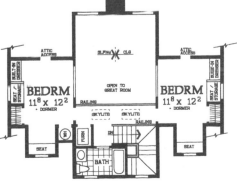

Quote One®

Cost to build? See page 188
to order complete cost estimate
to build this house in your area!

DESIGN	M3674
BEDROOMS	3
BATHROOMS	2
FIRST FLOOR	1,086 Sq. Ft.
SECOND FLOOR	554 Sq. Ft.
TOTAL	1,640 Sq. Ft.
PRICE	B2

This home's simple rectangular plan means relatively economical construction costs. Formal areas are located to the front of the plan. Each of the major living areas has direct access to wraparound porch. The living room is free of annoying cross-room traffic. It even has good blank wall space for effective furniture placement. Upstairs are three bedrooms and a bath with twin lavatories for the kids and a deluxe master suite with a lavish bath. For the development of additional recreational and storage space there is the basement.

WIDTH 56'
DEPTH 42'

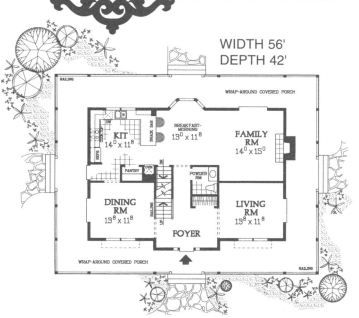

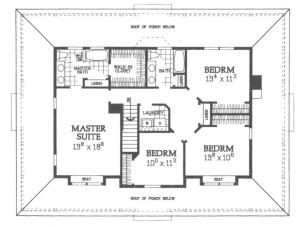

DESIGN M3653
BEDROOMS 4
BATHROOMS 2½
FIRST FLOOR 1,216 Sq. Ft.
SECOND FLOOR 1,191 Sq. Ft.
TOTAL 2,407 Sq. Ft.
PRICE B3

QUOTE ONE®

Cost to build? See page 188
to order complete cost estimate
to build this house in your area!

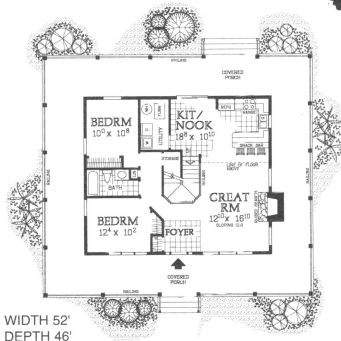

WIDTH 52'
DEPTH 46'

QUOTE ONE®
Cost to build? See page 188
to order complete cost estimate
to build this house in your area!

Here's a great country farmhouse with a lot of contemporary appeal. The generous use of windows—including two sets of triple muntin windows in the front—adds exciting visual elements to the exterior as well as plenty of natural light to the interior. An impressive tiled entry opens to a two-story great room with a raised hearth and views to the front and side grounds. The U-shaped kitchen conveniently combines with this area and offers a snack counter in addition to a casual dining nook with rear porch access. The family bedrooms reside on the main floor, while an expansive master suite with adjacent study creates a resplendent retreat upstairs, complete with a private balcony, walk-in closet and pampering bath.

DESIGN	M3681
BEDROOMS	3
BATHROOMS	2
FIRST FLOOR	1,093 Sq. Ft.
SECOND FLOOR	576 Sq. Ft.
TOTAL	1,669 Sq. Ft.
PRICE	B2

This board-and-batten Farmhouse has all of the country charm you're looking for. The large front covered porch will be appreciated during warm-weather months. Immediately off the front entrance is the delightful corner living room. The dining room with bay window will be easily served by the U-shaped kitchen. Informal family living takes place in the family room with raised-hearth fireplace, sliding glass doors to the rear terrace, and easy access to the powder room, laundry room and service entrance. The second floor has three bedrooms and two full baths. The master has a dormer and walk-in closet. Two other bedrooms share the second bath.

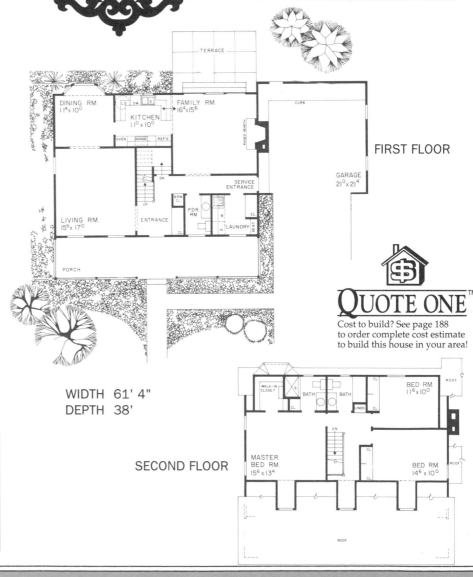

FIRST FLOOR

QUOTE ONE™

Cost to build? See page 188 to order complete cost estimate to build this house in your area!

WIDTH 61' 4"
DEPTH 38'

SECOND FLOOR

DESIGN	M2776
BEDROOMS	3
BATHROOMS	2½
FIRST FLOOR	1,134 Sq. Ft.
SECOND FLOOR	874 Sq. Ft.
TOTAL	2,008 Sq. Ft.
PRICE	B2

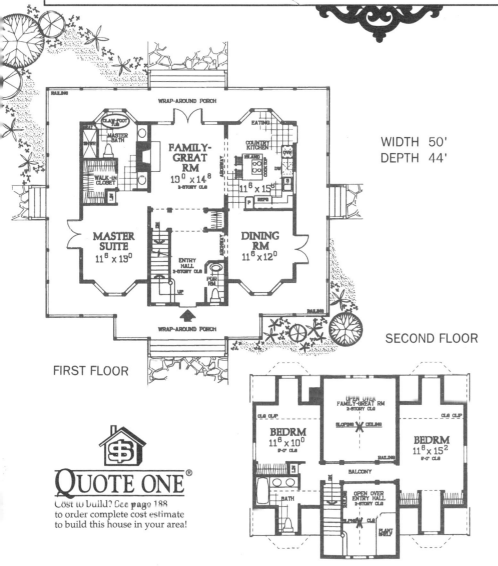

WIDTH 50'
DEPTH 44'

FIRST FLOOR

SECOND FLOOR

There's nothing that tops gracious Southern hospitality—unless its offered Southern Farmhouse Style! Here, the wraparound porch extends an invitation to enjoy gentle summer breezes and a refreshing glass of iced mint tea. The entry hall soars two stories, opening through an archway on the right to a banquet-sized formal dining room. Nearby, the efficient country kitchen shares space with a bay-windowed eating area. The two story family/great room enjoys a warming fireplace in the winter and is open to outdoor country comfort through French doors in the summer. The first-floor master suite offers a window seat, a dressing area and access to the wrap around porch. The second floor holds two family bedrooms which share a full bath. Plans for an optional indoor swimming pool/spa and detached garage are included.

QUOTE ONE®

Cost to build? See page 188 to order complete cost estimate to build this house in your area!

DESIGN	M3619
BEDROOMS	3
BATHROOMS	2½
FIRST FLOOR	1,171 Sq. Ft.
SECOND FLOOR	600 Sq. Ft.
TOTAL	1,771 Sq. Ft.
PRICE	B2

Rustic charm abounds in this pleasant Farmhouse rendition. Covered porches to the front and rear enclose living potential for the whole family. Flanking the entrance foyer are the living and dining rooms. Each is large enough to handle both casual and formal entertaining. To the rear is the L-shaped kitchen with island cook top and snack bar. A small family room/breakfast nook is attached for very informal activities. A private study is tucked away on this floor next to the master suite. On the second floor are three bedrooms and a full bath. Two of the bedrooms have charming dormer windows.

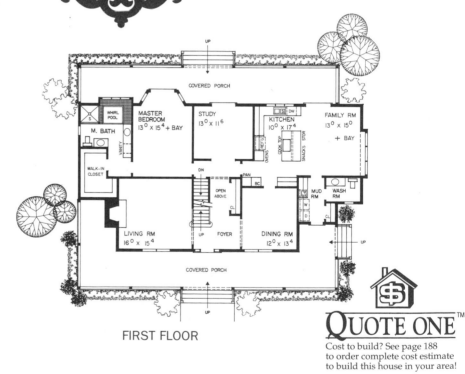

FIRST FLOOR

QUOTE ONE™

Cost to build? See page 188 to order complete cost estimate to build this house in your area!

SECOND FLOOR

DESIGN	M3396
BEDROOMS	4
BATHROOMS	2½
FIRST FLOOR	1,829 Sq. Ft.
SECOND FLOOR	947 Sq. Ft.
TOTAL	2,776 Sq. Ft.
PRICE	B3

WIDTH 62'
DEPTH 48' 8"

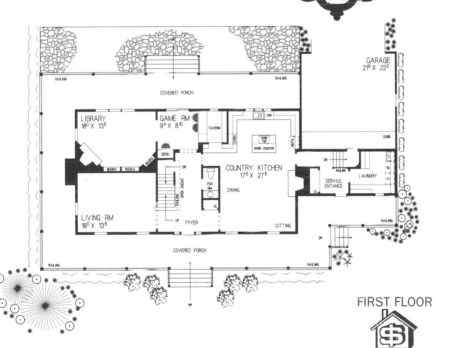

FIRST FLOOR

This is the ultimate in farmhouse living—six dormer windows and a porch that stretches essentially around the entire house. Inside the plan is open and inviting. Besides the large country kitchen with fireplace, there is a small game room with attached tavern, a library with built-in bookshelves and a fireplace and a formal living room. The second floor has four bedrooms and three full baths. Note the separate His and Hers walk-in closets and the whirlpool spa in the master suite bath. The service entrance features a mud room and laundry area conveniently just off the garage.

Quote One™

Cost to build? See page 188 to order complete cost estimate to build this house in your area!

SECOND FLOOR

DESIGN	M3399
BEDROOMS	4
BATHROOMS	3½
FIRST FLOOR	1,716 Sq. Ft.
SECOND FLOOR	2,102 Sq. Ft.
TOTAL	3,818 Sq. Ft.
PRICE	B4

WIDTH 82'
DEPTH 49' 8"

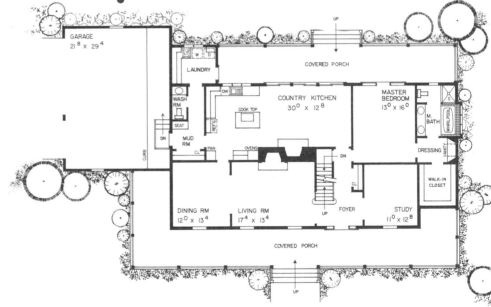

Five second-story dormers and a wide covered front porch add to the country charm of this Farmhouse design. Inside, an open floor plan offers great livability. The entry foyer opens to the left to a formal living room with fireplace and attached dining room. To the right is a private study. The back of the plan is dominated by a huge country kitchen featuring an island cook top and access to the rear covered porch. On this floor is the master suite with dual lavatories and a large walk-in closet. The second floor holds three bedrooms (or two and a sitting room) with two full baths. The dormers add interest to rooms on this floor.

California Engineered Plans and California Stock Plans are available for this home. Call 1-800-521-6797 for more information.

FIRST FLOOR

SECOND FLOOR

WIDTH 82'
DEPTH 50'

DESIGN	M3397
BEDROOMS	3 or 4
	(sitting room)
BATHROOMS	3½
FIRST FLOOR	1,855 Sq. Ft.
SECOND FLOOR	1,241 Sq. Ft.
TOTAL	3,096 Sq. Ft.
PRICE	B4

FIRST FLOOR

SECOND FLOOR

QUOTE ONE™

Cost to build? See page 188
to order complete cost estimate
to build this house in your area!

With its classic Farmhouse good-looks and just-right floor plan, this country residence has it all. The wraparound covered porch at the entry gives way to a long foyer with open staircase. To the right and left are the formal dining room and the living room. More casual living areas are to the rear: a family room and U-shaped kitchen with attached breakfast room. A covered porch at the back is reached by two sets of sliding glass doors. The second floor holds sleeping areas—two family bedrooms and a huge master suite with walk-in closet and pampering master bath. Special amenities include an ample laundry area, large walk-in pantry and corner fireplaces in both living areas.

DESIGN	M3398
BEDROOMS	3
BATHROOMS	2½
FIRST FLOOR	1,533 Sq. Ft.
SECOND FLOOR	1,288 Sq. Ft.
TOTAL	2,821 Sq. Ft.
PRICE	B3

WIDTH 92'
DEPTH 44'

Our Neo-Classic Farmhouse offers plenty of room for delightful diversions; a sheet-metal roof adds old-fashioned flair; front and rear porches accommodate out-of-doors lounging. Inside, a large living area with fireplace affords grand lounging; a dining room, cozy interludes. A fully functional kitchen, powder room and utility room round out the first floor. The second floor provides well-arranged sleeping quarters—with large master bedroom—and two full baths. Don't forget the interesting mud yard separating the garage from the house.

QUOTE ONE™

Cost to build? See page 188 to order complete cost estimate to build this house in your area!

DESIGN	M3469
BEDROOMS	3
BATHROOMS	2½
FIRST FLOOR	1,066 Sq. Ft.
SECOND FLOOR	1,006 Sq. Ft.
TOTAL	2,072 Sq. Ft.
PRICE	B2

COVERED PORCH

DINING RM.
$11^0 \times 13^2$
9' CLG

KITCHEN
$13^0 \times 13^2$
9' CLG

PANTRY

LIVING ROOM
$19^6 \times 17^{10}$
9' CLG

PWDR. RM.

FOYER

GARAGE
$21^4 \times 20^8$

STOR

STOR

DN

DN

DN

UP

COVERED PORCH

FIRST FLOOR

WIDTH 70' 4"
DEPTH 50' 4"

SECOND FLOOR

BEDROOM
$13^0 \times 11^2$
8' CLG

BEDROOM
$13^0 \times 11^2$
8' CLG

BATH

LINEN

W.I.C.

MASTER BATH

MASTER BEDROOM
$15^6 \times 15^6$
8' CLG

OPEN BELOW

DN

COVERED BALCONY

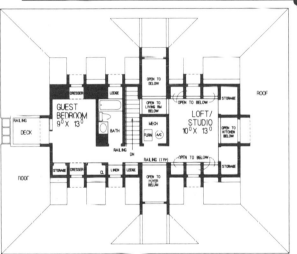

WIDTH 59'
DEPTH 30'

SECOND FLOOR

A unique Farmhouse plan which provides a grand floor plan, this home is comfortable in country or suburban settings. Formal entertaining areas share first-floor space with family gathering rooms and work and service areas. The master suite is also on this floor for convenience and privacy. Upstairs is a guest bedroom, private bath and loft area that makes a perfect studio. The covered porches front and rear lend outdoor appeal. Don't miss the deck off the upstairs guest bedroom. Other special features make this a great place to come home to.

Quote One™

Cost to build? See page 188 to order complete cost estimate to build this house in your area!

FIRST FLOOR

DESIGN	M3438
BEDROOMS	2 or 3
BATHROOMS	3
FIRST FLOOR	1,489 Sq. Ft.
SECOND FLOOR	741 Sq. Ft.
TOTAL	2,230 Sq. Ft.
PRICE	B3

There's nothing lacking in this Contemporary Farmhouse. A wrap-around porch ensures a favorite spot for enjoying good weather. A large great room sports a fireplace and lots of natural light. Grab a snack at the kitchen island/snack bar or in the bright breakfast room. The vaulted foyer grandly introduces the dining room and sitting parlor—the master bedroom is just off this room. Inside it: tray ceiling, fireplace, luxury bath and walk-in closet. Stairs lead up to a quaint loft/bedroom—perfect for study or snoozing—a full bath and an additional bedroom. Designated storage space also makes this one a winner.

FIRST FLOOR

SECOND FLOOR

QUOTE ONE™

Cost to build? See page 188 to order complete cost estimate to build this house in your area!

WIDTH 85' 2"
DEPTH 49' 2"

DESIGN	M3468
BEDROOMS	3
BATHROOMS	2½
FIRST FLOOR	1,618 Sq. Ft.
SECOND FLOOR	510 Sq. Ft.
TOTAL	2,128 Sq. Ft.
PRICE	B2

Decidedly different, this Neo-Classical Farmhouse offers more than just great looks. Interesting angles come into play in the front-facing living areas with dormer windows and curving walls. French doors lead to a rear covered patio. The living room's fireplace also services the master bedroom. A compartmented bath, walk-in closet and private access to the wrapping covered porch complete the appeal of this bedroom. At the opposite end of the house, a U-shaped kitchen with a round end counter that benefits the nook, a laundry room and a second bedroom complete the plan. Outside, a built-in barbecue lends special appeal to the porch.

QUOTE ONE™
Cost to build? See page 188
to order complete cost estimate
to build this house in your area!

WIDTH 89'
DEPTH 46' 2"

DESIGN	M3466
BEDROOMS	2
BATHROOMS	2
SQUARE FOOTAGE	1,800
PRICE	B2

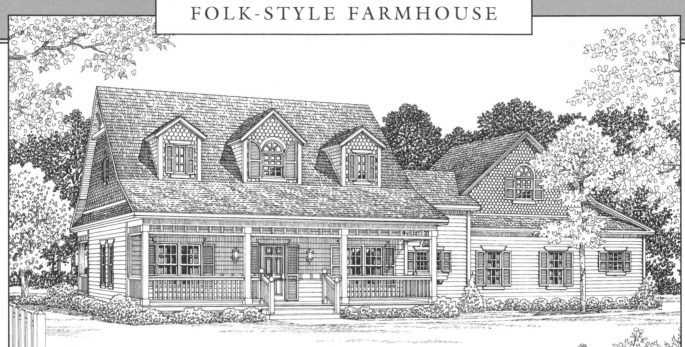

Gabled dormers accentuate the facade of this classic farmhouse. The covered front porch is a perfect spot for enjoying cool evening breezes. Inside, this home's layout provides privacy for both the homeowner and the family. The children's bedrooms are found on the left of the foyer and share a full bath with dual vanities. To the right of the foyer is the formal dining room. The angular great room offers a raised-hearth fireplace with an accommodating media shelf. The central, U-shaped kitchen is easily accessible from any room and opens up to a sun-drenched morning room. The private master suite is impressive with its access to the sun patio, large walk-in closet and luxurious bath.

WIDTH 76'
DEPTH 64'

QUOTE ONE®

Cost to build? See page 188
to order complete cost estimate
to build this house in your area!

DESIGN	M3677
BEDROOMS	3
BATHROOMS	2½
SQUARE FOOTAGE	2,090
PRICE	B2

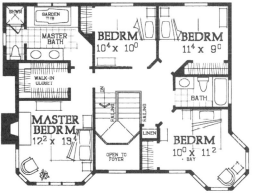

QUOTE ONE®

Cost to build? See page 188
to order complete cost estimate
to build this house in your area!

WIDTH 72'
DEPTH 50'-10"

Victorian style is highly evident on this beautiful four-bedroom, two-story home. With fish-scale trim, a turret skirted by an octagonal porch and varied window treatments, this home is a true winner. The interior continues with a cozy octagonal study, a spacious living room complete with a warming fireplace, a formal dining room which offers access to the rear porch, and a large and efficient kitchen that shares a snack bar with the comfortable family room. The sleeping zone is contained upstairs and consists of three secondary bedrooms—one in the top of the tower—that share a full hall bath, and a lavish master suite. This suite pampers with a fireplace, a large walk-in closet and a sumptuous bath.

DESIGN	M3696
BEDROOMS	4
BATHROOMS	2½
FIRST FLOOR	1,186 Sq. Ft.
SECOND FLOOR	988 Sq. Ft.
TOTAL	2,174 Sq. Ft.
PRICE	B2

HOME PLANNERS

Each set of blueprints is an interrelated collection of plans, measurements, drawings and diagrams showing precisely how your house comes together. Here's what the package includes:

- FRONTAL SHEET. An artist's landscaped sketch of the exterior along with inkline floor plans.
- FOUNDATION PLAN. A complete basement and foundation plan drawn to ¼-inch scale, plus a sample plot plan for locating your house on a building site.
- DETAILED FLOOR PLANS. Drawn to ¼-inch scale, each floor plan includes cross-section detail keys and layouts of electrical outlets and switches.
- HOUSE CROSS-SECTIONS. Large-scale interior details show key sections of the foundation, interior and exterior walls, floors and roof details.

- INTERIOR ELEVATIONS. Large-scale interior details show the design of kitchen cabinets, bathrooms, laundry areas, fireplaces and built-ins.
- EXTERIOR ELEVATIONS. Drawings in ¼-inch scale show the front, rear and sides of your house.

SPECIFICATION OUTLINE. Available separately from the blueprint package, this handy 16-page, fill-in-the-blanks document contains more than 150 stages crucial to the construction of your home. A handy guide and record, it allows you to pinpoint building materials, equipment and methods of construction.

MATERIALS LIST. Also available separately, this customized materials list specifies the quantity, type and size of material needed to build your house (with the exception of mechanical-system items).

PRICES

The blueprints you order are a master plan for building your new home. Even the smallest house in the Home Planners' portfolio is a complicated combination of construction and architectural data. Bigger houses, irregularly shaped houses and houses with an abundance of design features are even more complex and require proportionately greater resources to design and develop. The price schedule below takes these factors into account.

	B1	B2	B3	B4	B5
One-set Study Package	$350	$390	$430	$470	$590
Four-set Building Package	$395	$435	$475	$515	$635
Eight-set Building Package	$455	$495	$535	$575	$695
One-set Reproducible Sepias	$555	$615	$675	$735	$795
Home Customizer® Package	$605	$665	$725	$785	$845

Additional Identical Blueprints in same order $50 per set
Reverse Blueprints (Mirror-Image) $50 per set
Specification Outlines $10 each

MATERIALS LISTS

Schedule B1-B4 $50 each
Schedule B5 $60 each
Additional Materials Lists in same order $10 each

For additional information about our plans, Quote One® Cost Estimating Service, Custom Engineering Service, Home Customizer® Package, and California Engineered Plans, please call 1-800-521-6797 or 520-297-8200.

TO ORDER BLUEPRINTS, TURN TO PAGE 187.

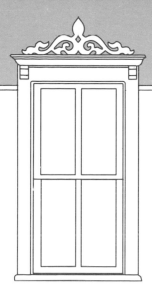

HISTORICAL REPLICATIONS, INC.

In 1977, while living in Atlanta, Cecilia Reese Bullock began a construction company that specialized in building traditional houses. One day a visitor to her job site complimented Bullock on her imaginative incorporation of architectural antiques in the new homes she was building—but lamented the shortage of actual old houses available for purchase and renovation.

"Suddenly I had an idea," Bullock recalls. "If there were not enough old houses for old-house lovers—why not meet the needs of this market by building new houses that retained the exact proportions and details of historic homes—yet incorporated all the latest technological advances in a floor plan updated for modern lifestyles?"

Bullock began planning her next construction project: an exact copy of an 1855 antebellum Farmhouse that she had long admired. She decided to build a replica of this historic home and test her design concept in the heavily attended Home Expo (The Atlanta Homebuilders' Association Parade of Homes).

Bullock remembers that the response to the home was overwhelming. Throughout the entire Expo, long lines remained constant in front of the house. "My doubts were resolved: there was a very receptive and very appreciative market for new houses that were identical to old houses."

Shortly after the Home Expo, Bullock's husband was unexpectedly transferred to Jackson, Mississippi. "As soon as I completed my building projects in Atlanta, I joined my husband in Jackson. I had decided to pursue the historical house-plan concept in earnest. With the assistance of artists, draftsmen and designers both in Jackson and Atlanta, I developed twenty-four Victorian and Farmhouse designs. This first portfolio was so well received that I soon enlarged it to include forty-eight designs. And, even though we are known nationally as specialists in Victorian architecture, over the past decade we have developed three other portfolios in Acadian, Greek Revival, Georgian and Federal styles."

Bullock increasingly had to expand her staff to accommodate the demand for alterations and custom designs. "Even though I had originally planned to offer only stock plans, I had so many requests for custom designs that I could not ignore the fact that there was a need for specialized plans to meet individualized needs."

Historical Replications has studied Victorians from San Francisco to Savannah and taken countless photographs to insure that its design and drafting staff use only authentic details. Owners have reported that visitors—and on occasion, subcontractors—have mistaken their new house for a skillful renovation of an old one.

Over the past ten years, Historical Replications has seen its designs featured in most major building magazines. *Traditional Building* magazine described Cecilia Reese Bullock as the person "who has had more influence than any other single individual in making historical American architecture popular in the new housing market." In 1990, Bullock was recognized for her contributions to American residential architecture in the prestigious British documentary series "Hooray for Today, USA."

Comments Bullock: "Historical Replications is dedicated to developing designs that preserve not only the ambience but the *quality* of homes of the past era. And though our floor plans incorporate the latest amenities, our houses convey the feeling of a beloved old home. They create an emotional, nostalgic response."

QUEEN ANNE COTTAGE

With a facade and floor plan reminiscent of an earlier era, this charming Victorian house unobtrusively incorporates such modern amenities as a powder room, a separate breakfast bay and a walk-through laundry room. The foyer opens onto a well-proportioned great room with a wood-burning fireplace. A large cased opening leads to the adjacent dining room. A double tier of windows illuminates the dramatic stairwell, which leads up to three bedrooms. The master suite is carefully zoned away from the other two bedrooms; it contains a compartmentalized dressing area and an oversized closet. The luxurious master bath features His and Hers vanities. Plans for the detached garages for this home can be seen on pages 176 and 177.

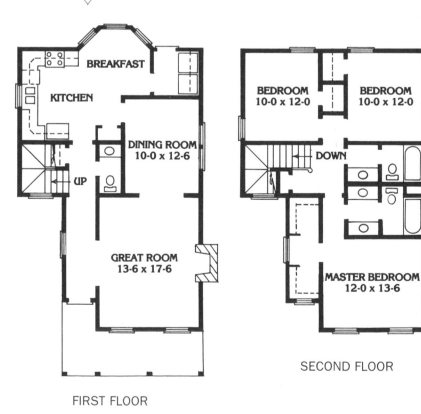

BREAKFAST

KITCHEN

DINING ROOM
10-0 x 12-6

UP

GREAT ROOM
13-6 x 17-6

FIRST FLOOR

BEDROOM
10-0 x 12-0

BEDROOM
10-0 x 12-0

DOWN

MASTER BEDROOM
12-0 x 13-6

SECOND FLOOR

DESIGN	M8800
BEDROOMS	3
BATHROOMS	2½
FIRST FLOOR	846 Sq. Ft.
SECOND FLOOR	784 Sq. Ft.
TOTAL	1,630 Sq. Ft.
PRICE	C1

WIDTH 27'
DEPTH 47'

FOLK VICTORIAN COTTAGE

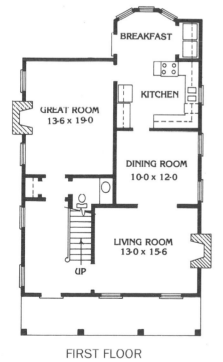

FIRST FLOOR

BREAKFAST

KITCHEN

GREAT ROOM
13-6 x 19-0

DINING ROOM
10-0 x 12-0

LIVING ROOM
13-0 x 15-6

UP

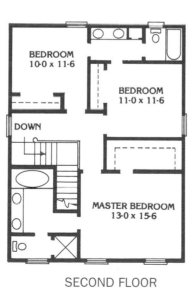

SECOND FLOOR

BEDROOM
10-0 x 11-6

BEDROOM
11-0 x 11-6

DOWN

MASTER BEDROOM
13-0 x 15-6

The inviting porch of this charming turn-of-the-century house extends a gracious welcome. The expansive foyer opens onto both the living room and great room, which contain fireplaces. A formal dining room is conveniently situated between the living room and the kitchen, and is well located for entertaining. The master bedroom has a bath with a double vanity and a separate shower stall, as well as an oversized whirlpool tub. A large walk in closet completes the amenities of this spacious room. The other bedrooms open directly into a compartmentalized bath with another double vanity. This house is especially suitable for a narrow lot and is compatible with a detached garage, plans for which can be seen on pages 176 and 177.

WIDTH 31'
DEPTH 50'

DESIGN	M8801
BEDROOMS	3
BATHROOMS	2½
FIRST FLOOR	1,066 Sq. Ft.
SECOND FLOOR	913 Sq. Ft.
TOTAL	1,979 Sq. Ft.
PRICE	C1

This delightful Victorian design is an updated version of an authentic turn-of-the-century design. Originally offered in George Barber's 1890 plan book, *The Cottage Souvenir #3*, this appealing house readily adapts itself to a more modern floor plan. The expansive kitchen, with an attached island and breakfast bar, is a welcome addition to the original plan. A walk-in utility room, located conveniently near the kitchen, facilitates laundry chores. A cozy fireplace warms the great room. The second-floor master suite features a walk-in closet, a separate sitting area and a large master bath with individual vanities. Both bedrooms contain generous walk-in closets. Plans for detached garages for this home can be seen on pages 176 and 177.

FIRST FLOOR

SECOND FLOOR

WIDTH 30'
DEPTH 34'

DESIGN	M8802
BEDROOMS	2
BATHROOMS	2½
FIRST FLOOR	828 Sq. Ft.
SECOND FLOOR	700 Sq. Ft.
TOTAL	1,528 Sq. Ft.
PRICE	C1

FOLK VICTORIAN

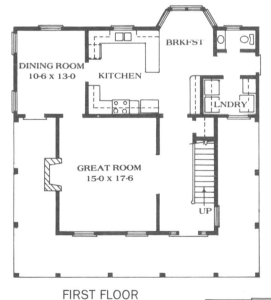

FIRST FLOOR

DINING ROOM
10-6 x 13-0

KITCHEN

BRKFST

LNDRY

GREAT ROOM
15-0 x 17-6

UP

WIDTH 38'
DEPTH 42'

SECOND FLOOR

BEDROOM
10-6 x 13-0

BEDROOM
11-0 x 13-0

DOWN

MASTER
BEDROOM
13-0 x 14-0

Undeniably appealing, the wraparound porch of this engaging dwelling lends additional warmth to a very special house plan. Within, a graceful stairway rises from a spacious foyer and is brightened through thoughtful window placement. The great room features a fireplace and plenty of space for entertaining. The adjoining formal dining room opens onto a sheltered porch. Additional seating space for less formal dining is offered in the large breakfast bay. Nearby, a built-in cabinet provides shelves for cookbooks and cherished serving pieces. Upstairs floorspace is especially well-utilized. A minimum amount of hallway is used to provide access to the three bedrooms. The master suite has a partitioned bath and a separate tub and shower. Plans for detached garages for this home can be seen on pages 176 and 177.

DESIGN	M8806
BEDROOMS	3
BATHROOMS	2½
FIRST FLOOR	1,005 Sq. Ft.
SECOND FLOOR	846 Sq. Ft.
TOTAL	1,851 Sq. Ft.
PRICE	C1

FOLK VICTORIAN COTTAGE

This nostalgic house is an adaptation of the common T-shaped Farmhouses that ornament the nation's countryside. The front door is encircled by glass sidelights and a transom that contribute light to the sparkling entryway. An especially spacious great room is well-lit from long windows that, when opened, will provide ample air circulation on moderate days. A step-in pantry allows plenty of storage space for the cook who likes to shop ahead. On the second floor, an open railing overlooks the stairs below. The master bath includes a whirlpool tub and a separate shower. Plans for detached garages for this home can be seen on pages 176 and 177.

GREAT ROOM 14-0 x 20-6

KITCHEN

UP

DINING ROOM 11-0 x 13-0

FIRST FLOOR

DOWN

BEDROOM 9-0 x 11-0

MASTER BEDROOM 11-6 x 14-0

BEDROOM 9-6 x 11-0

SECOND FLOOR

DESIGN	M8804
BEDROOMS	3
BATHROOMS	2½
FIRST FLOOR	907 Sq. Ft.
SECOND FLOOR	785 Sq. Ft.
TOTAL	1,692 Sq. Ft.
PRICE	C1

WIDTH 36'
DEPTH 31'

FIRST FLOOR

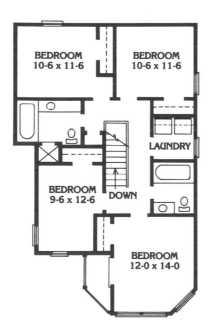

SECOND FLOOR

WIDTH 29'
DEPTH 46'

Well suited for a narrow lot, this splendid home contains authentic Queen Anne detailing with an asymmetrical façade and dominant front-facing gable. Within, a very open floor plan furnishes the right setting for today's more informal lifestyles. A first-floor master suite offers plenty of privacy in this five-bedroom home. On the second floor, the bedroom at the top of the stairs could easily be adapted to serve as a playroom or study. The front bedroom on the second floor has a balcony that could easily be enclosed if a more spacious bedroom is desired. This versatile plan is perfect for the larger family desiring an affordably priced house. Plans for detached garages for this home can be seen on pages 176 and 177.

DESIGN	M8811
BEDROOMS	5
BATHROOMS	3½
FIRST FLOOR	1,026 Sq. Ft.
SECOND FLOOR	937 Sq. Ft.
TOTAL	1,963 Sq. Ft.
PRICE	C1

The lacy and decorative ornamentation of this romantic cottage is a commonly observed feature of homes of the Victorian era. The bayed dining room on the front of the house echoes the original floor plan; but the up-to-date kitchen with its convenient breakfast bar introduces the latest technologic advances. A long, narrow pantry provides ample storage for food and for odd-size serving pieces. The first-floor master suite is a most welcome feature. The master bath features His and Hers vanities, as well as both a tub and separate shower. Upstairs, three spacious bedrooms house large closets. Additional storage space is provided in the walk-out attic. Plans for detached garages for this home can be seen on pages 176 and 177.

FIRST FLOOR

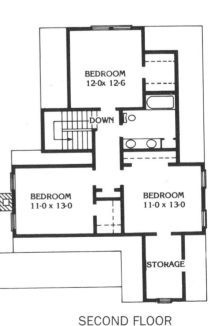

SECOND FLOOR

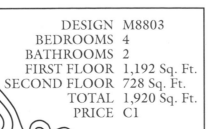

DESIGN M8803
BEDROOMS 4
BATHROOMS 2
FIRST FLOOR 1,192 Sq. Ft.
SECOND FLOOR 728 Sq. Ft.
TOTAL 1,920 Sq. Ft.
PRICE C1

WIDTH 35'
DEPTH 46'

QUEEN ANNE

FIRST FLOOR

BREAKFAST

GREAT ROOM
14-6 x 18-6

UP

KITCHEN

DINING ROOM
11-0 x 12-0

MASTER
BEDROOM
12-6 x 14-6

Some houses possess more than their fair share of warmth and charm, and this captivating design belongs in that category. The wraparound porch is a design element that is irresistibly inviting. A front-facing gable with fishscale shingles and gingerbread ornament imparts additional excitement. The master bedroom, located on the first floor, features a super-sized closet. A pass-through from the kitchen to the great room includes the cook in the midst of family life. Ascending conveniently from the great room, the stairs lead up to three bedrooms. A spacious dressing area with two separate vanities and multiple linen closets makes sharing a bath easy. Plans for detached garages for this home can be seen on pages 176 and 177.

BEDROOM
11-0 x 11-0

BEDROOM
11-0 x 12-6

DOWN

SECOND FLOOR

BEDROOM
11-0 x 12-6

WIDTH 44'
DEPTH 51'

DESIGN	M8810
BEDROOMS	4
BATHROOMS	2½
FIRST FLOOR	1,240 Sq. Ft.
SECOND FLOOR	718 Sq. Ft.
TOTAL	1,958 Sq. Ft.
PRICE	C1

With its bedazzling windows and intricate exterior details, this spirited Queen Anne residence proclaims its San Francisco heritage. The foyer is open to the second-floor ceiling, creating additional pizazz. Niches are built into the cased opening that leads into the dining room, providing an opportunity to display beloved collections. Openness is achieved with an oversized kitchen, bayed breakfast nook and commodious great room with fireplace. On the second floor, both family bedrooms have walk-in closets and individual vanities; one also features a bay window. The master bedroom suite provides the utmost privacy with its compartmentalized bath. Plans for detached garages for this home can be seen on pages 176 and 177.

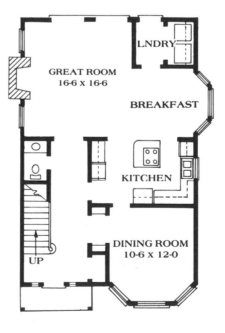

FIRST FLOOR

SECOND FLOOR

DESIGN	M8808
BEDROOMS	3
BATHROOMS	2½
FIRST FLOOR	1,019 Sq. Ft.
SECOND FLOOR	931 Sq. Ft.
TOTAL	1,950 Sq. Ft.
PRICE	C1

WIDTH 30'
DEPTH 42'

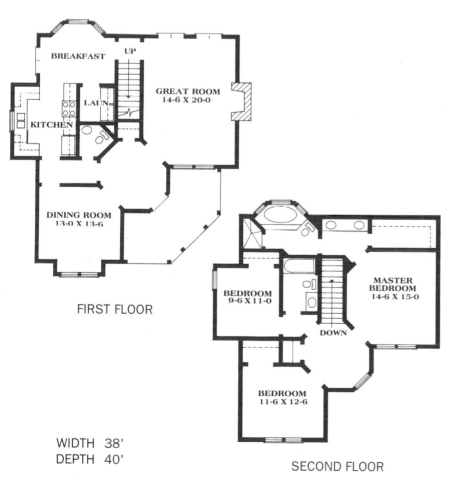

BREAKFAST

UP

KITCHEN

LAUN.

GREAT ROOM
14-6 X 20-0

DINING ROOM
13-0 X 13-6

FIRST FLOOR

BEDROOM
9-6 X 11-0

MASTER BEDROOM
14-6 X 15-0

DOWN

BEDROOM
11-6 X 12-6

SECOND FLOOR

WIDTH 38'

DEPTH 40'

The octagonal foyer of this Queen Anne Style house sets the pace for this enticing Victorian design. This spacious foyer leads to a formal dining room of expansive proportions, and also opens into a great room warmed by a wood-burning fireplace. The stairway arises conveniently near family living areas and ends on a second-floor landing that echoes the octagonal foyer below. Upstairs, a sumptuous master suite features a dazzling bath with a step-up whirlpool tub and separate shower. The oversized master closet contributes ample storage for clothes and accessories. Plans for detached garages for this home can be seen on pages 176 and 177.

DESIGN	M8809
BEDROOMS	3
BATHROOMS	2½
FIRST FLOOR	999 Sq. Ft.
SECOND FLOOR	948 Sq. Ft.
TOTAL	1,947 Sq. Ft.
PRICE	C1

The homes of the Victorian era contain indisputably the most interesting foyers of any architectural period. Frequently, these entry rooms were large enough to serve as auxiliary living spaces for the large families that occupied them. The bayed foyer of this authentic Queen Anne design is ample enough for a cozy sitting area, or, furnished with a desk, a spot for a convenient study. Directly over the foyer, the master bath repeats the bay windows below. This sumptuous bath features an enormous amount of counter space, as well as a whirlpool tub and separate shower. A laundry chute in the master closet places clothes in the huge laundry room directly below. Plans for detached garages for this home can be seen on pages 176 and 177.

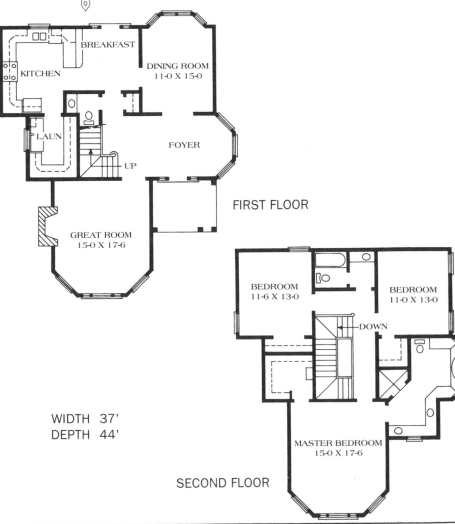

FIRST FLOOR

SECOND FLOOR

WIDTH 37'
DEPTH 44'

DESIGN	M8812
BEDROOMS	3
BATHROOMS	2½
FIRST FLOOR	1,118 Sq. Ft.
SECOND FLOOR	1,040 Sq. Ft.
TOTAL	2,158 Sq. Ft.
PRICE	C2

GREAT ROOM
15-0 x 19-0

KITCHEN

LAUN

UP

DINING ROOM
11-6 x 14-6

FIRST FLOOR

Especially suited for a narrow lot, this winning design proclaims its Victorian heritage with appropriately detailed window trim and gable ornaments. A beveled-glass front door opens into a foyer which is illuminated by the three windows on the stairwell. The generous kitchen offers both a breakfast bar on the island and a breakfast nook with built-in seating, if desired. The spacious master bedroom suite features His and Hers walk-in closets. The large master bath with its garden tub is dazzling. Plans for detached garages for this home can be seen on pages 176 and 177.

SECOND FLOOR

BEDROOM
10-6 x 13-0

BEDROOM
11-0 x 13-6

DOWN

MASTER BEDROOM
14-6 x 15-6

WIDTH 31'
DEPTH 36'

DESIGN	M8813
BEDROOMS	3
BATHROOMS	2½
FIRST FLOOR	991 Sq. Ft.
SECOND FLOOR	895 Sq. Ft.
TOTAL	1,886 Sq. Ft.
PRICE	C1

An immense great room is the focal
point of this appealing dwelling. This
room leads into a large dining room
and adjacent kitchen. The long
breakfast bar will appeal to families
who must catch a quick meal on the
run. Nearby, a back entry opens onto
a powder room and a walk-through
laundry room, a location important to
families who need a mudroom as they
enter the house. The expansive great
room contains a fireplace. The first-
floor master suite is isolated from the
three upstairs bedrooms. An oversized tub is a notable feature of the
compartmentalized bathroom, as well
as a separate shower and His and
Hers vanities. Plans for detached
garages for this home can be seen on
pages 176 and 177.

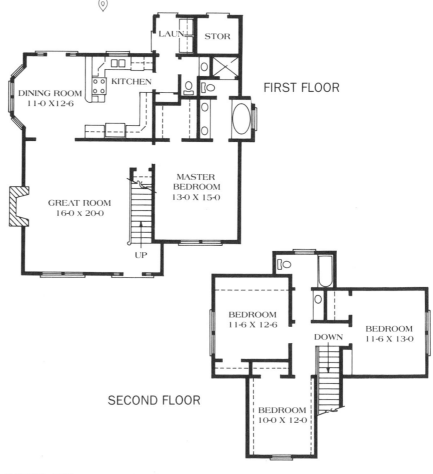

FIRST FLOOR

SECOND FLOOR

DESIGN	M8814
BEDROOMS	4
BATHROOMS	2½
FIRST FLOOR	1,168 Sq. Ft.
SECOND FLOOR	672 Sq. Ft.
TOTAL	1,840 Sq. Ft.
PRICE	C1

WIDTH 38'
DEPTH 40'

BREAKFAST

DINING ROOM
12-0 x 13-6

KITCHEN

FIRST FLOOR

GREAT ROOM
14-0 x 19-0

MASTER BEDROOM
12-6 x 18-6

UP

SECOND FLOOR

BEDROOM
11-6 x 12-6

SITTING AREA

DOWN

BEDROOM
12-6 x 15-6

OPEN TO BELOW

WIDTH 44'
DEPTH 40'

The front-facing pediment with authentic Victorian sunburst ornamentation crowns the entryway with its oval beveled-glass door. The vaulted or coved ceiling of the great room and dining room contributes a feeling of spaciousness to rooms already generous in proportion. A kitchen with long counters and tall cabinets is adjacent to a walk-in laundry and a deep pantry. The first-floor master suite is exceptionally roomy and contains a compartmentalized bath and walk-in closet. The second-floor bedrooms feature large closets and share a cozy sitting area at the top of the open stairway. Plans for detached garages for this home can be seen on pages 176 and 177.

DESIGN	M8815
BEDROOMS	3
BATHROOMS	2½
FIRST FLOOR	1,424 Sq. Ft.
SECOND FLOOR	689 Sq. Ft.
TOTAL	2,113 Sq. Ft.
PRICE	C2

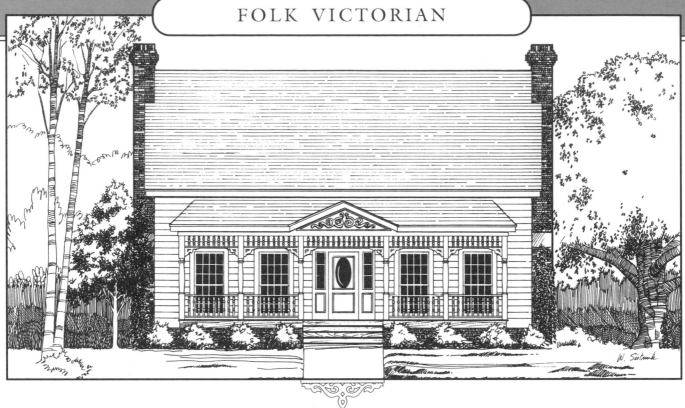

The front porch of this charming Victorian design, with its turned columns and graceful fretwork, emanates a warm welcome to all who enter. Within, this unpretentious design offers a very open floor plan for those who enjoy a casual lifestyle. The kitchen, breakfast area, and cozy keeping area with fireplace are all one large room. On the opposite side of the center hall, another lengthy room provides the opportunity for additional living and dining areas. A first-floor master suite with a walk-in closet offers both convenience and quiet seclusion. Two second-floor bedrooms share a spacious bath with a double vanity. Plans for detached garages for this home can be seen on pages 176 and 177.

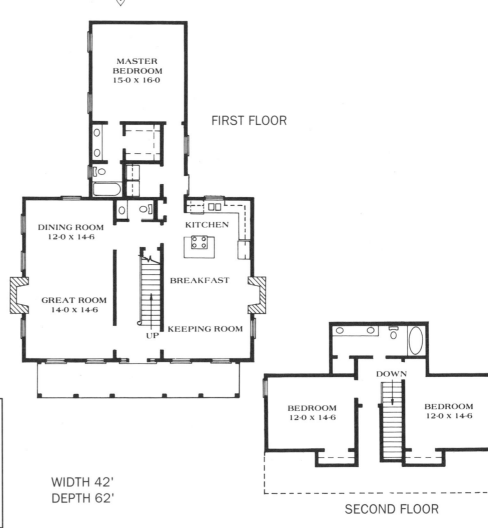

FIRST FLOOR

MASTER BEDROOM
15-0 x 16-0

DINING ROOM
12-0 x 14-6

KITCHEN

BREAKFAST

GREAT ROOM
14-0 x 14-6

KEEPING ROOM

UP

SECOND FLOOR

DOWN

BEDROOM
12-0 x 14-6

BEDROOM
12-0 x 14-6

WIDTH 42'
DEPTH 62'

DESIGN	M8805
BEDROOMS	3
BATHROOMS	2½
FIRST FLOOR	1,490 Sq. Ft.
SECOND FLOOR	610 Sq. Ft.
TOTAL	2,100 Sq. Ft.
PRICE	C2

SECOND FLOOR

BEDROOM
11-6 x 12-0

DOWN

BEDROOM
12-0 x 13-6

STORAGE

STORAGE

FIRST FLOOR

BREAKFAST

KITCHEN

MASTER
BEDROOM
14-0 x 17-0

GREAT ROOM
15-6 x 19-6

UP

DINING ROOM
13-0 x 14-6

WIDTH 48'
DEPTH 40'

Asymmetry of facade is a characteristic Victorian feature. Differing wall textures, such as the change from lap siding to fishscale shingles on the front-facing gable, is another distinguishing architectural trait. This inviting dwelling opens into a foyer sparkling with light from a stained-glass window on the stair landing above. A formal dining room and a great room provide ample space for holiday festivities. A secluded first-floor master suite offers a handsome bath with dual vanities, separate shower and walk-in closet. Above are two family bedrooms with private baths. A large storage area may be completed and used as a fourth bedroom or a recreational area. Plans for detached garages for this home can be seen on pages 176 and 177.

DESIGN	M8820
BEDROOMS	3 or 4
BATHROOMS	3½
FIRST FLOOR	1,582 Sq. Ft.
SECOND FLOOR	720 Sq. Ft.
TOTAL	2,302 Sq. Ft.
PRICE	C2

Perfect for a narrow lot, this compact design restates its Victorian heritage with a graceful wraparound veranda. The bracketed fretwork which connects the simple columns and frames the long front windows is authentic turn-of-the-century enhancement. An extra-spacious foyer offers access to the long and wide great room and adjacent dining room, which are separated by a generous cased opening. The interior fretwork used here is typical of the period. The breakfast and dining rooms are each flooded with light from their many windows. A large laundry room has a utility sink and plenty of counter space for folding clothes. Above, the commodious master suite features a whirlpool tub crowned with a Palladian window. Each of the bedrooms has a walk-in closet. Plans for detached garages for this home can be seen on pages 176 and 177.

FIRST FLOOR

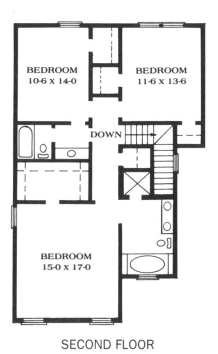

SECOND FLOOR

DESIGN	M8816	
BEDROOMS	3	
BATHROOMS	2½	
FIRST FLOOR	1,107 Sq. Ft.	
SECOND FLOOR	1,039 Sq. Ft.	
TOTAL	2,146 Sq. Ft.	
PRICE	C2	

WIDTH 31'
DEPTH 50'

FIRST FLOOR

LAUNDRY

BREAKFAST

GREAT ROOM
14-6 x 15-0

KITCHEN

UP

DINING ROOM
11-0 x 13-6

LIVING ROOM
10-0 x 17-0

WIDTH 30'
DEPTH 45'

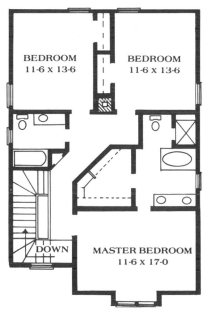

BEDROOM
11-6 x 13-6

BEDROOM
11-6 x 13-6

DOWN

MASTER BEDROOM
11-6 x 17-0

SECOND FLOOR

Adapted from Bicknell's *Detail Cottage and Construction Architecture,* published in 1873, this delightful Victorian residence readily adapts to an up-to-date floor plan. The chief adornment of the elegant foyer is an open stairway. The lengthy formal living room is connected to a spacious dining room, providing excellent circulation for families who enjoy frequent entertaining. The bayed great room contains plans for a built-in bookcase and media center, as well as a closet for game or hobby storage. The open kitchen features a center island with range and a bayed breakfast area. Upstairs, the master suite features a roomy bath with tub and shower and an oversized closet. Plans for detached garages for this home can be seen on pages 176 and 177.

DESIGN	M8817
BEDROOMS	3
BATHROOMS	2½
FIRST FLOOR	1,105 Sq. Ft.
SECOND FLOOR	979 Sq. Ft.
TOTAL	2,084 Sq. Ft.
PRICE	C2

QUEEN ANNE

The exuberant visual display created by this delectable Queen Anne design heralds its Victorian heritage. Transom-topped windows accurately reflect the love of views and veneration of sunlight of this era. Inside, a sizable foyer leads into both formal and informal areas. A spacious great room is amply illuminated by a bay encircled with windows. It opens into a sunlit breakfast area that adjoins a well-appointed kitchen with island cooktop. The walk-through laundry is convenient to the kitchen and the outdoors. Above, a capacious master suite has both a whirlpool tub and an elongated shower. The other two bedrooms each have a bay window. Plans for detached garages for this home can be seen on pages 176 and 177.

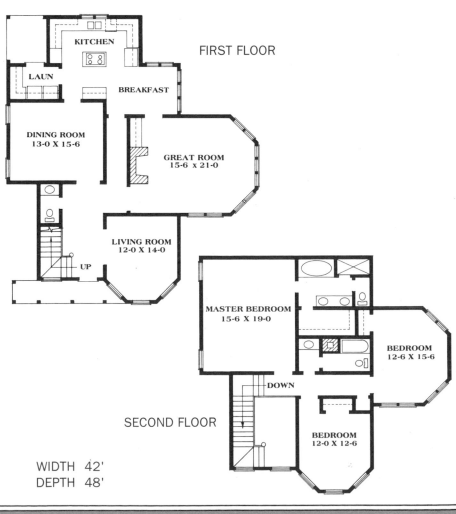

DESIGN M8823
BEDROOMS 3
BATHROOMS 2½
FIRST FLOOR 1,325 Sq. Ft.
SECOND FLOOR 1,052 Sq. Ft.
TOTAL 2,377 Sq. Ft.
PRICE C2

WIDTH 42'
DEPTH 48'

FOLK VICTORIAN

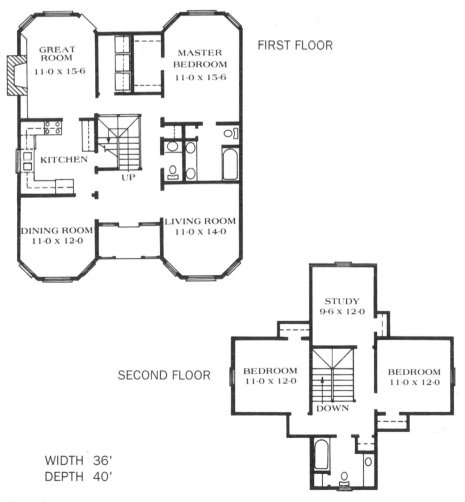

FIRST FLOOR

GREAT ROOM
11·0 X 15·6

MASTER BEDROOM
11·0 X 15·6

KITCHEN

UP

DINING ROOM
11·0 X 12·0

LIVING ROOM
11·0 X 14·0

SECOND FLOOR

STUDY
9·6 X 12·0

BEDROOM
11·0 X 12·0

BEDROOM
11·0 X 12·0

DOWN

WIDTH 36'
DEPTH 40'

This multi-gabled Victorian achieves a formal interior in a compact amount of space. Its nearly square shape makes it surprisingly economical to construct as well as to heat and cool. Four bay windows impart light and drama to the downstairs rooms. An open foyer with an elegant stairwell opens into spacious rooms. The great room features a fireplace and a door to the outside. Zoned quietly away from the noise of family living, the roomy master suite has a bay-windowed sitting area and a spacious bath. Above, two additional bedrooms share a study or a playroom, which could double as a guest room if additional sleeping space is required. Plans for detached garages for this home can be seen on pages 176 and 177.

DESIGN	M8807
BEDROOMS	3 or 4 (study)
BATHROOMS	2½
FIRST FLOOR	1,217 Sq. Ft.
SECOND FLOOR	620 Sq. Ft.
TOTAL	1,837 Sq. Ft.
PRICE	C1

QUEEN ANNE

The popular Victorian architect, Shoppell, was the progenitor of this delightful design; the exterior of this house is faithfully reproduced from his book of house plans, *Turn of the Century Houses, Cottages, and Villas*. The sheltering front porch provides cover for the front door and wraps around to provide access to a handy kitchen door. A wide foyer leads to an expansive great room. Just beyond the great room, the dining room connects to the spacious kitchen and breakfast area. Right above the rear porch, a private terrace opens off the master bedroom. The master bath features a large walk-in closet, a double vanity, and separate tub and shower. Two additional bedrooms share a partitioned bath. Plans for detached garages for this home can be seen on pages 176 and 177.

DESIGN	M8818
BEDROOMS	3
BATHROOMS	2½
FIRST FLOOR	1,085 Sq. Ft.
SECOND FLOOR	1,090 Sq. Ft.
TOTAL	2,175 Sq. Ft.
PRICE	C2

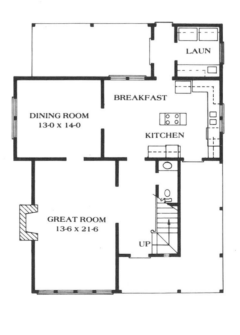

FIRST FLOOR

LAUN

BREAKFAST

DINING ROOM
13-0 x 14-0

KITCHEN

GREAT ROOM
13-6 x 21-6

UP

MASTER
BEDROOM
13-0 x 16-6

BEDROOM
11-0 x 13-0

DOWN

SECOND FLOOR

BEDROOM
13-0 x 13-6

WIDTH 35'
DEPTH 45'

QUEEN ANNE

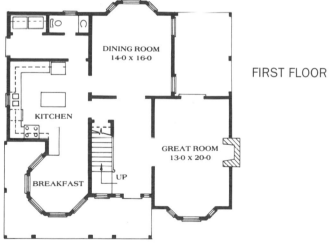

FIRST FLOOR

DINING ROOM
14-0 x 16-0

KITCHEN

GREAT ROOM
13-0 x 20-0

BREAKFAST

UP

SECOND FLOOR

BEDROOM
12-0 x 14-0

BEDROOM
12-0 x 14-0

DOWN

MASTER
BEDROOM
13-0 x 20-0

WIDTH 42'
DEPTH 42'

Sparkling like a jewel with its many beveled-glass transoms, this enticing Queen Anne Victorian delivers the enchantment of living in an authentic turn-of-the-century home. The octagonal tower is surrounded by a wraparound porch featuring the delicate spindlework common to this era. Within, a wide foyer provides a glimpse of the bayed dining room. A rear porch is located behind the great room. An exceptionally large kitchen with a center island opens into the octagonal breakfast bay. On the second floor, the master bath has a step-up whirlpool tub. A private terrace opening off the master suite provides an opportunity for outdoor living, or, if glassed-in, a secluded study. Plans for detached garages for this home can be seen on pages 176 and 177.

DESIGN	M8819
BEDROOMS	3
BATHROOMS	2½
FIRST FLOOR	1,148 Sq. Ft.
SECOND FLOOR	1,095 Sq. Ft.
TOTAL	2,243 Sq. Ft.
PRICE	C2

The lacy spindlework and corner bracket detailing of the inviting front porch announce the Queen Anne heritage of this enchanting design. From the foyer, a U-shaped stairway with a landing window rises gracefully. The living room provides a secluded spot away from the noise of family living, and could easily serve as a quiet study. The roomy kitchen with its work island is connected to a large dining room by a butler's pantry. If desired, a wet bar could be installed here. Above, a generously sized master bedroom offers such amenities as a whirlpool tub and elongated shower stall. Plans for detached garages for this home can be seen on pages 176 and 177.

FIRST FLOOR

BREAKFAST

KITCHEN   LAUN

DINING ROOM
13-0 X 15-0

GREAT ROOM
15-0 X 18-0

UP

LIVING
ROOM
11-0 X 13-0

SECOND FLOOR

BEDROOM
13-0 X 14-6

MASTER BEDROOM
13-0 X 18-0

BEDROOM
11-0 X 13-0

DESIGN	M8822
BEDROOMS	3
BATHROOMS	2½
FIRST FLOOR	1,259 Sq. Ft.
SECOND FLOOR	1,025 Sq. Ft.
TOTAL	2,284 Sq. Ft.
PRICE	C2

WIDTH 42'
DEPTH 44'

FOLK VICTORIAN

FIRST FLOOR

BREAKFAST

GREAT ROOM
16-0 x 20-6

KITCHEN

DINING ROOM
12-0 x 14-0

UP

GUEST BEDROOM
12-0 x 13-0

This warm and charming house, with its hipped-roof double dormer, is a nostalgic tribute to a beloved architectural era. An inviting porch leads into a traditional foyer; to the left, a spacious dining room opens onto a well-designed kitchen. The great room is warmed by a fireplace flanked with built-in bookcases. The first-floor guest bedroom could also serve as a quiet study. Above, the master bedroom suite includes separate His and Hers closets. The sumptuous master bath has a step-up tub and an oversized shower stall. The two upstairs bedrooms, each with its own walk-in closet, share a luxurious compartmentalized bath featuring separate dressing areas with vanities. Plans for detached garages for this home can be seen on pages 176 and 177.

MASTER BEDROOM
13-0 x 17-0

LAUNDRY

DOWN

SECOND FLOOR

BEDROOM
12-0 x 13-6

BEDROOM
12-0 x 13-6

WIDTH 34'
DEPTH 54'

DESIGN	M8826
BEDROOMS	4
BATHROOMS	3
FIRST FLOOR	1,224 Sq. Ft.
SECOND FLOOR	1,174 Sq. Ft.
TOTAL	2,398 Sq. Ft.
PRICE	C2

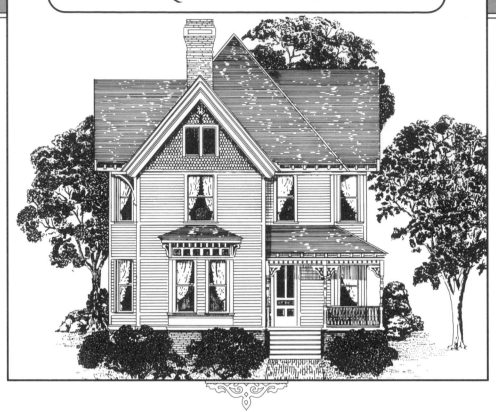

Adapted from the 1890 house plan book *The Cottage Souvenir #2* by the renowned Victorian architect, George Barber, this design graces streets in all parts of the country. Its familiar Queen Anne roof line features a steeply pitched hip roof of irregular shape, with a dominant front-facing gable. Another authentic feature is the wraparound veranda. This updated rendition is perfect for a narrow lot. Formal living and dining areas offer privacy from the family living spaces. The bayed great room features a fireplace with built-in shelves on each side. Above, the master suite contains a bayed sitting area, a walk-in closet and a luxurious bath. The other upstairs bedrooms are exceptionally spacious as well. Plans for detached garages for this home can be seen on pages 176 and 177.

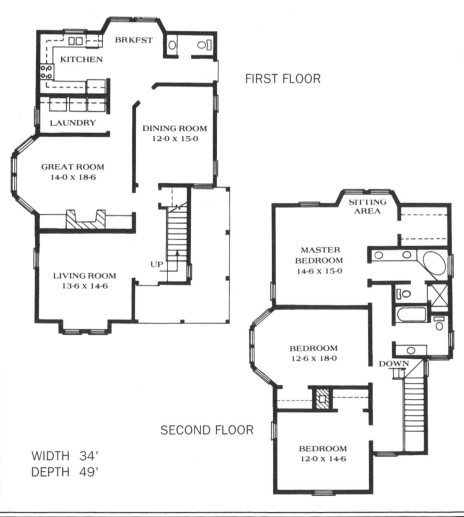

FIRST FLOOR

SECOND FLOOR

DESIGN	M8821
BEDROOMS	3
BATHROOMS	2½
FIRST FLOOR	1,188 Sq. Ft.
SECOND FLOOR	1,133 Sq. Ft.
TOTAL	2,321 Sq. Ft.
PRICE	C2

WIDTH 34'
DEPTH 49'

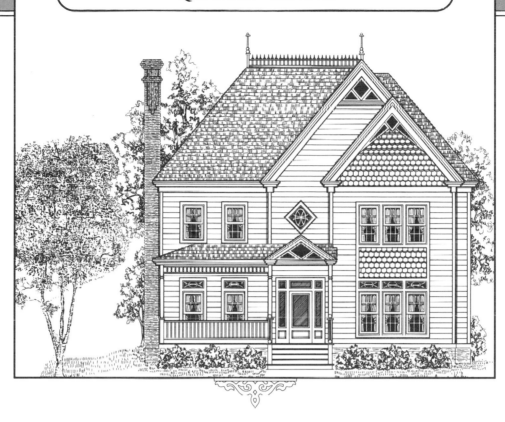

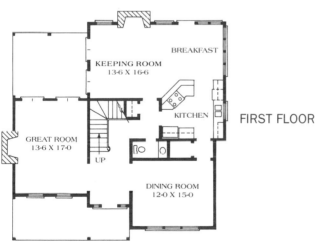

FIRST FLOOR

KEEPING ROOM
13-6 X 16-6

BREAKFAST

KITCHEN

GREAT ROOM
13-6 X 17-0

UP

DINING ROOM
12-0 X 15-0

SECOND FLOOR

BEDROOM
11-0 X 13-0

BEDROOM
11-6 X 13-0

DOWN

MASTER
BEDROOM
13-6 X 17-0

LAUN

BEDROOM
12-0 X 15-0

WIDTH 42'
DEPTH 42'

The front-facing gables of this hipped-roof Queen Anne, complete with detailed gable ornamentation, proclaim the authenticity of this resplendent design. The pedimented entryway is another architectural characteristic of the Victorian era. Within, a roomy foyer opens into a great room that is flanked by both front and rear porches. The kitchen provides an angled breakfast bar and a cozy keeping room for family members who like to gather during meal preparation. Above, four spacious bedrooms are zoned quietly away from family living. The master suite provides a partitioned bath and walk-in closet. The second-floor laundry saves many a trip up and down the stairs. Plans for detached garages for this home can be seen on pages 176 and 177.

DESIGN	M8827
BEDROOMS	4
BATHROOMS	3½
FIRST FLOOR	1,176 Sq. Ft.
SECOND FLOOR	1,278 Sq. Ft.
TOTAL	2,454 Sq. Ft.
PRICE	C2

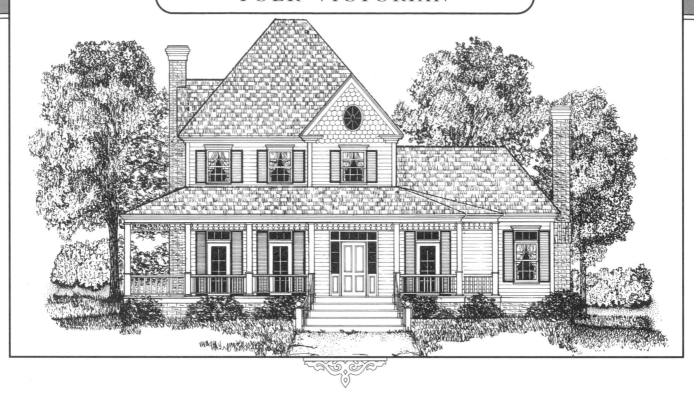

Porches that wrap around the outside of a house add special warmth and welcome to the exterior appearance. This appealing dwelling continues its gracious statement with an inviting living room and adjoining dining room. The exceptionally large great room provides a central area for family living, well away from these quieter areas. A country kitchen with a large center work island and breakfast bar allows plenty of company for the family cook. The spacious utility room with a separate laundry sink is convenient to the outdoors and can function as a mudroom. On the second floor, the master suite provides a walk-in closet, separate tub and shower and a double vanity. Plans for detached garages for this home can be seen on pages 176 and 177.

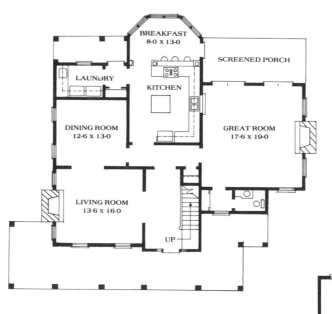

FIRST FLOOR

BREAKFAST
8-0 x 13-0

SCREENED PORCH

LAUNDRY

KITCHEN

DINING ROOM
12-6 x 13-0

GREAT ROOM
17-6 x 19-0

LIVING ROOM
13-6 x 16-0

UP

DESIGN	M8824
BEDROOMS	3
BATHROOMS	2½
FIRST FLOOR	1,476 Sq. Ft.
SECOND FLOOR	912 Sq. Ft.
TOTAL	2,388 Sq. Ft.
PRICE	C2

WIDTH 58'
DEPTH 51'

BEDROOM
10-0 x 13-0

BEDROOM
10-0 x 13-0

DOWN

MASTER BEDROOM
12-6 x 16-0

SECOND FLOOR

FIRST FLOOR

KITCHEN · LAUNDRY

BREAKFAST · PANTRY

GREAT ROOM
14-6 x 18-0

UP

DINING ROOM
12-0 x 12-6

LIVING ROOM
12-0 x 15-0

MASTER
BEDROOM
12-6 x 16-6

SECOND FLOOR

BEDROOM
10-0 x 12-6

BEDROOM
12-0 x 15-6

DOWN

BEDROOM
10-0 x 12-6

WIDTH 45'
DEPTH 54'

Queen Anne houses, with their projecting bays, towers and wrap-around porches, are the apex of the Victorian era. This up-to-date rendition of the beloved style captures a floor plan that is as dramatic within as without. The front-facing pediment ornamented with typical gable detailing highlights the front doorway and provides additional welcome to this enchanting abode. The angles and bays that occur in every first-floor room add visual excitement to formal and informal living and dining areas. A well-lit breakfast bay with its soaring ceiling is a spectacular addition to this classic plan. The first-floor master suite features two walk-in closets. Three upstairs bedrooms also have spacious walk-in closets. Plans for detached garages for this home can be seen on pages 176 and 177.

DESIGN	M8825
BEDROOMS	4
BATHROOMS	3½
FIRST FLOOR	1,600 Sq. Ft.
SECOND FLOOR	790 Sq. Ft.
TOTAL	2,390 Sq. Ft.
PRICE	C2

One of the hallmarks of authentic Victorian architecture is a profusion of windows in a variety of styles. Turn-of-the-century homebuilders repeatedly produced architectural excitement through the creative use of window glass. The transom-topped and side-lighted front door leads into a foyer; a beveled-glass window from the stair landing far above casts jewel-like tones into the area below. An expansive great room has a separate nook that occupies the base of the tower. A covered rear porch provides outdoor living space. Upstairs, the master bedroom also utilizes the tower to provide a separate sitting area. The other two bedrooms are connected via a compartmentalized bath. Plans for detached garages for this home can be seen on pages 176 and 177.

DESIGN	M8828
BEDROOMS	3
BATHROOMS	2½
FIRST FLOOR	1,349 Sq. Ft.
SECOND FLOOR	1,170 Sq. Ft.
TOTAL	2,519 Sq. Ft.
PRICE	C2

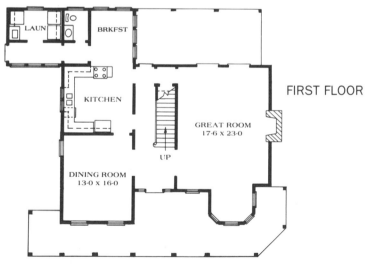

FIRST FLOOR

LAUN

BRKFST

KITCHEN

GREAT ROOM
17-6 x 23-0

UP

DINING ROOM
13-0 x 16-0

BEDROOM
12-0 x 13-0

SECOND FLOOR

DOWN

MASTER BEDROOM
13-6 x 17-6

BEDROOM
12-0 x 13-0

WIDTH   54'
DEPTH   47'

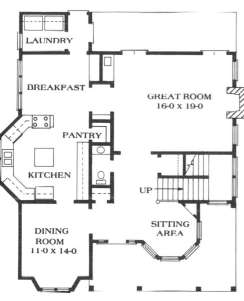

LAUNDRY

BREAKFAST

GREAT ROOM
16-0 x 19-0

PANTRY

KITCHEN

UP

FIRST FLOOR

DINING
ROOM
11-0 x 14-0

SITTING
AREA

SECOND FLOOR

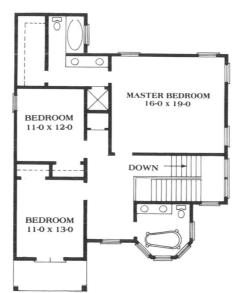

MASTER BEDROOM
16-0 x 19-0

BEDROOM
11-0 x 12-0

DOWN

BEDROOM
11-0 x 13-0

WIDTH 44'
DEPTH 46'

The 1878 edition of *Bicknell's Victo-rian Buildings* inspired the intricate window casings and porch details of this dazzling residence. A tower large enough for a sitting area lends instant impact to the foyer. A charming niche, suitable for either cookbooks or collectibles, is tucked between the great room and breakfast area; a glassed-door hutch built into the breakfast room provides additional space for storage and display. The bayed kitchen with work island and walk-in pantry provides all the latest amenities. Above, the guest bath-room with an elevated ceiling and claw-footed tub occupies the second floor of the tower. A super-sized master bedroom features a compart-mentalized bath and a roomy walk-in closet. Plans for detached garages for this home can be seen on pages 176 and 177.

DESIGN	M8829
BEDROOMS	3
BATHROOMS	2½
FIRST FLOOR	1,259 Sq. Ft.
SECOND FLOOR	1,181 Sq. Ft.
TOTAL	2,440 Sq. Ft.
PRICE	C2

George Barber's *The Cottage Souvenir #2* provided the inspiration for this faithful replica of a Victorian era home. The integral (recessed) second-floor porch is an important feature of homes of this vintage. Additionally, the pedimented entryway is a predominant characteristic of Queen Anne architecture. Within, most rooms contain large bays which contribute light and excitement. The spacious kitchen opens onto an oversized dining nook which leads into a huge utility room, ample enough for a freezer. An elegant open stairway leads to the second-floor bedrooms. The master suite is warmed by a wood-burning fireplace. Plans for detached garages for this home can be seen on pages 176 and 177.

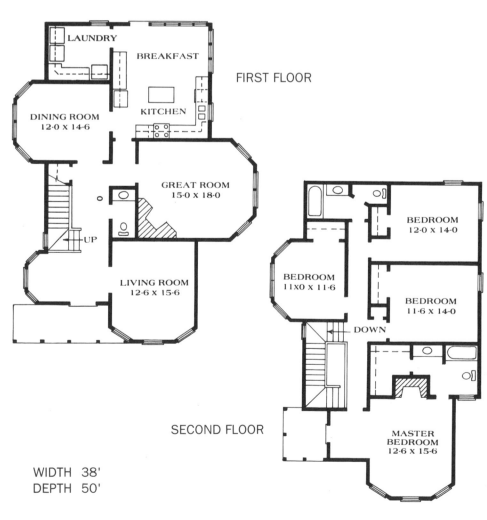

FIRST FLOOR

LAUNDRY

BREAKFAST

KITCHEN

DINING ROOM
12-0 x 14-6

GREAT ROOM
15-0 x 18-0

UP

LIVING ROOM
12-6 x 15-6

BEDROOM
12-0 x 14-0

BEDROOM
11x0 x 11-6

BEDROOM
11-6 x 14-0

DOWN

SECOND FLOOR

MASTER
BEDROOM
12-6 x 15-6

DESIGN	M8830
BEDROOMS	4
BATHROOMS	2½
FIRST FLOOR	1,408 Sq. Ft.
SECOND FLOOR	1,194 Sq. Ft.
TOTAL	2,602 Sq. Ft.
PRICE	C2

WIDTH 38'
DEPTH 50'

FIRST FLOOR

LAUN

GREAT ROOM
15-6 x 17-6

BREAKFAST

LIVING ROOM
11-6 x 15-0

KITCHEN

UP

DINING ROOM
11-6 x 17-6

SECOND FLOOR

BEDROOM
12-0 x 15-6

BEDROOM
11-6 x 13-0

DOWN

SITTING
AREA

MASTER BEDROOM
13-0 x 17-6

WIDTH 52'
DEPTH 51'

This breathtaking Queen Anne Victorian home features a spectacular wraparound porch that culminates in an octagonal pavilion, ideal for gatherings on pleasant days. This shape is repeated in the tower that arises from the center of the house. An elongated dining room easily holds a multi-leaved table; a thoroughly up-to-date kitchen overlooks the great room. The formal living room may be converted to a guest room with only a little rearranging. Above, the master suite contains a partitioned sitting area. Its opulent bath has an unusual amount of built-in storage. All upstairs bedrooms contain walk-in closets. Plans for detached garages for this home can be seen on pages 176 and 177.

DESIGN	M8831
BEDROOMS	3
BATHROOMS	2 ½
FIRST FLOOR	1,364 Sq. Ft.
SECOND FLOOR	1,283 Sq. Ft.
TOTAL	2,647 Sq. Ft.
PRICE	C2

A wraparound porch and an octagonal tower are authentic details of this Queen Anne home. High-ceilinged rooms, with angles and bays, accurately reflect the Victorian love of unpredictability and whimsy. The expansive kitchen has a center work island; it leads into a window-encircled breakfast bay. The dining room is planned so that its beautifully arrayed table is visible from the foyer. On the second floor, two of the three hall bedrooms share a compartmentalized bath with separate vanities; the third has a private bath. The lengthy master suite has ample room for a sitting area. Its full bath features a sumptuous step-up whirlpool tub. Plans for detached garages for this home can be seen on pages 176 and 177.

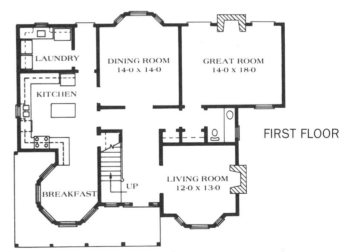

FIRST FLOOR

LAUNDRY

DINING ROOM
14-0 X 14-0

GREAT ROOM
14-0 X 18-0

KITCHEN

LIVING ROOM
12-0 X 13-0

BREAKFAST   UP

SECOND FLOOR

BEDROOM
12-0 X 14-0

BEDROOM
12-0 X 14-0

BEDROOM
11-6 X 14-0

DOWN

MASTER
BEDROOM
13-0 X 18-6

DESIGN	M8832
BEDROOMS	4
BATHROOMS	3½
FIRST FLOOR	1,417 Sq. Ft.
SECOND FLOOR	1,380 Sq. Ft.
TOTAL	2,797 Sq. Ft.
PRICE	C2

WIDTH 51'
DEPTH 42'

FOLK VICTORIAN

GREAT ROOM
17-0 x 25-0

FIRST FLOOR

LAUNDRY   KITCHEN

BEDROOM
12-0 x 14-0

UP   DINING ROOM
12-0 x 14-0

This beguiling Victorian home, with its double tier of porches, features a dramatic pair of Palladian windows. These graceful windows flood the foyer and the second-floor landing with glittering light. The foyer contains a striking stairway, angled to repeat the entryway. The first-floor bedroom can be adapted for use as a study or library if needed. The spacious kitchen has a built-in dining nook; beyond, a commodious great room opens onto a deep and shady porch. Upstairs, the master bedroom is warmed by a cheery fireplace; it opens onto a private second-floor terrace. Each bedroom in this plan has a private bath. Plans for detached garages for this home can be seen on pages 176 and 177.

SECOND FLOOR

MASTER BEDROOM
17-0 x 25-0

DOWN

BEDROOM
12-0 x 14-0

OPEN

BEDROOM
12-0 x 13-0

WIDTH 48'
DEPTH 49'

DESIGN	M8833
BEDROOMS	4
BATHROOMS	4
FIRST FLOOR	1,390 Sq. Ft.
SECOND FLOOR	1,292 Sq. Ft.
TOTAL	2,682 Sq. Ft.
PRICE	C2

Doubled classical columns set on pedestals are an unusual but authentic architectural detail found in the Victorian era. Inside, an especially spacious foyer displays a traditional L-shaped stairway with an open well. The extra width in the dining room accommodates cherished heirloom furniture; just beyond, the bayed kitchen with its large island is open to a sun-filled breakfast room/gallery. A deep back porch serves as additional space for out-of-doors living. The study can also function as a guest room with its own private bath. Upstairs, the elegant master suite has ample room for a sitting area; the bath has His and Hers walk-in closets. Plans for detached garages for this home can be seen on pages 176 and 177.

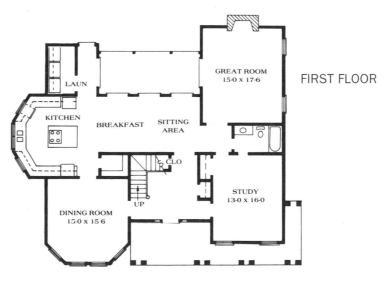

FIRST FLOOR

DESIGN	M8834
BEDROOMS	3
BATHROOMS	3
FIRST FLOOR	1,628 Sq. Ft.
SECOND FLOOR	1,179
TOTAL	2,807 Sq. Ft.
PRICE	C2

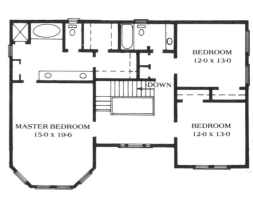

SECOND FLOOR

WIDTH 54'
DEPTH 47'

QUEEN ANNE

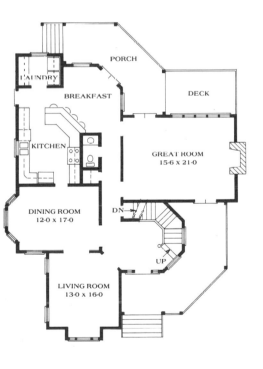

PORCH

LAUNDRY

BREAKFAST

DECK

FIRST FLOOR

KITCHEN

GREAT ROOM
15-6 x 21-0

DINING ROOM
12-0 x 17-0

DN→

UP

LIVING ROOM
13-0 x 16-0

MASTER BEDROOM
15-0 x 19-0

BATH

SECOND FLOOR

BEDROOM
12-0 x 15-0

DN

BATH

BEDROOM
13-0 x 14-0

WIDTH 45'
DEPTH 60'

Appreciators of the Victorian era will exult in the carefully preserved exterior details of this stunning house. A graceful veranda wraps around the charming facade, providing covered access to the foyer and to the great room. The angled foyer with repetitively shaped stairs is a popular 19th-Century feature. A super-sized dining room will accommodate a long table; the dramatically angled breakfast bay offers a second tantalizing place in which to dine. The double-tiered back porch eases the transition to the out-of-doors. Above, a master dressing suite contains two exceptional closets. The other bedrooms have a divided bath and walk-in closets. Plans for detached garages for this home can be found on pages 176 and 177.

DESIGN	M8835
BEDROOMS	3
BATHROOMS	2½
FIRST FLOOR	1,440 Sq. Ft.
SECOND FLOOR	1,358 Sq. Ft.
TOTAL	2,798 Sq. Ft.
PRICE	C2

FOLK VICTORIAN

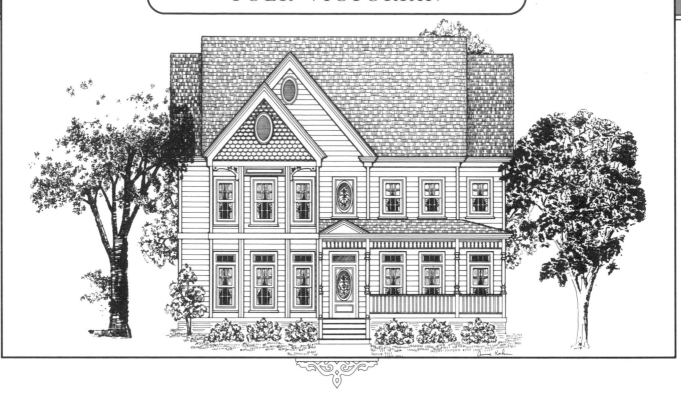

The two-storied bay that projects from the dominant front-facing gable of this Folk Victorian adds to its charm and elegance. The transom-topped oval-glassed door opens into a long foyer with U-shaped stairs. Beyond the formal living and dining rooms, the foyer leads to a spacious great room warmed by a fireplace that is flanked with French doors. The bay-windowed breakfast nook is adjacent to the well-planned kitchen. A first-floor guest suite offers privacy and seclusion. Above, three more bedrooms and a large master suite are also zoned for privacy. The master bedroom is particularly relaxing with its separate sitting area. Plans for detached garages for this home can be seen on pages 176 and 177.

FIRST FLOOR

SECOND FLOOR

WIDTH 44'
DEPTH 45'

DESIGN M8836
BEDROOMS 5
BATHROOMS 4
FIRST FLOOR 1,551 Sq. Ft.
SECOND FLOOR 1,422 Sq. Ft.
TOTAL 2,973 Sq. Ft.
PRICE C2

FIRST FLOOR

GREAT ROOM
15-0 x 20-0

BREAKFAST

GUEST BEDROOM
12-6 x 15-0

KITCHEN

LAUN

UP

DINING ROOM
13-0 x 16-6

SECOND FLOOR

BEDROOM
13-6 x 14-0

MASTER BEDROOM
15-0 x 18-0

DOWN

BEDROOM
13-0 x 15-6

WIDTH 53'
DEPTH 54'

The beckoning porch of this appealing dwelling has many authentic Victorian details, such as the double-tiered front-facing pediments that crown the first- and second-floor doors. The angled side entry onto the front porch is another architectural highlight. Once inside, the spaciousness of the foyer extends an instant welcome. An extra-long dining room features a dramatic bay. Just beyond, a well-appointed kitchen is at the center of family activities. The first-floor guest suite can serve as a study or hobby room, if desired. Upstairs, two large bedrooms have walk-in closets; the capacious master suite has His and Hers vanities and His and Hers closets. Plans for detached garages for this home can be seen on pages 176 and 177.

DESIGN	M8837
BEDROOMS	4
BATHROOMS	3½
FIRST FLOOR	1,534 Sq. Ft.
SECOND FLOOR	1,448 Sq. Ft.
TOTAL	2,982 Sq. Ft.
PRICE	C2

The inspiration for this spellbinding residence came from the beloved Victorian architect, George Barber. The lacy veranda that embraces the exterior of this enchanting home offers outdoor living space under its shady recesses. Within, spacious bayed rooms create additional pizazz, as well as contributing light and floor space. The roomy kitchen is chock-full of the latest amenities, including a sit-down bar on the long work island. A supersized utility room facilitates clothes-handling chores. On the floor above, an enormous master suite has a separate shower, whirlpool tub, and plenty of dressing space. The other three bedrooms have large closets, as well. Plans for detached garages for this home can be seen on pages 176 and 177.

FIRST FLOOR

SECOND FLOOR

WIDTH 56'
DEPTH 56'

DESIGN	M8838
BEDROOMS	4
BATHROOMS	2½
FIRST FLOOR	1,959 Sq. Ft.
SECOND FLOOR	1,765 Sq. Ft.
TOTAL	3,724 Sq. Ft.
PRICE	C3

FIRST FLOOR

LAUN

BREAKFAST

KITCHEN

KEEPING ROOM
15-6 x 15-6

DINING ROOM
12-0 X 13-6

UP

GUEST ROOM
11-0 X12-6

GREAT ROOM
15-0 X 19-0

SECOND FLOOR

BEDROOM
11-0 X 13-6

BEDROOM
12-6 X 13-6

BEDROOM
12-0 X 13-6

DOWN

UP

MASTER
BEDROOM
15-0 x 15-0

WIDTH 44'
DEPTH 55'

The decoratively rich facade of this lively Queen Anne house indicates a passion for Victorian authenticity. An impressive entryway is topped by a porch pediment that adds extra emphasis to the facade. Within, the intriguing stairway provides an opportunity for accuracy in Victorian millwork. The kitchen, however, is full of the most modern technologic advancements. The serious cook will appreciate the walk-in food closet and the butler's pantry that leads into the dining room. There is a first-floor guest suite; above, four other bedrooms easily accommodate the larger family. The master bedroom is the proud possessor of an elaborate bath located in the high-ceilinged tower. Plans for detached garages for this home can be seen on pages 176 and 177.

DESIGN	M8839
BEDROOMS	5
BATHROOMS	4
FIRST FLOOR	1,578 Sq. Ft.
SECOND FLOOR	1,418 Sq. Ft.
TOTAL	2,996 Sq. Ft.
PRICE	C2

This sparkling Victorian is encircled by a graceful porch with turned columns resting on elevated pedestals. A second-story porch creates additional interest and repeats the doubled columns below. Within, a resplendent foyer looks into an expansive great room and beyond to a spacious dining room. The enormous kitchen houses a second set of stairs to facilitate the flow of family traffic. The glass-encircled living room is zoned well away from the uproar of family life. On the second floor, four bedrooms have been planned. The master suite is particularly inviting, with its opulent bath and separate closets. The kitchen stairs originate conveniently near the back bedrooms. Plans for detached garages for this home can be seen on pages 176 and 177.

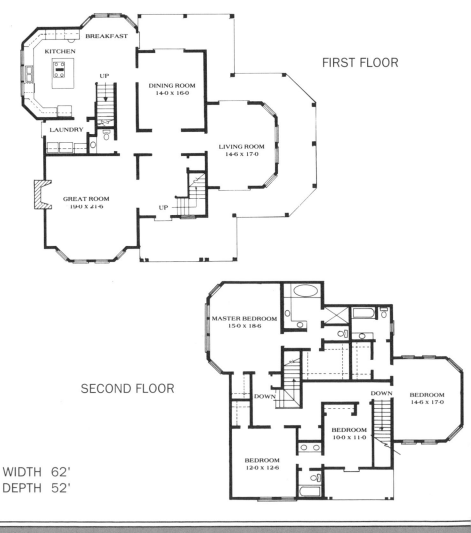

FIRST FLOOR

BREAKFAST

KITCHEN

UP

LAUNDRY

DINING ROOM
14-0 x 16-0

LIVING ROOM
14-6 x 17-0

GREAT ROOM
19-0 x 21-6

UP

SECOND FLOOR

MASTER BEDROOM
15-0 x 18-6

DOWN

DOWN

BEDROOM
14-6 x 17-0

BEDROOM
10-0 x 11-0

BEDROOM
12-0 x 12-6

DESIGN	M8840
BEDROOMS	4
BATHROOMS	3½
FIRST FLOOR	1,834 Sq. Ft.
SECOND FLOOR	1,664 Sq. Ft.
TOTAL	3,498 Sq. Ft.
PRICE	C3

WIDTH 62'
DEPTH 52'

FIRST FLOOR

GARAGE
24-0 x 24-0

BREAKFAST

KITCHEN

GREAT ROOM
15-0 x 26-0

UP

DINING ROOM
13-6 x 17-6

LIVING ROOM
13-0 x 16-0

SECOND FLOOR

STORAGE

BEDROOM
11-6 x 19-0

MASTER BEDROOM
15-0 x 21-0

LAUNDRY

UP

DOWN

BEDROOM
12-0 x 13-6

BEDROOM
13-0 x 14-0

WIDTH 48'
DEPTH 68'

The Italianate heritage of this imposing Victorian design is revealed in
such architectural elements as the
centered squared tower, the long
narrow windows, and its three-storied
appearance. The updated floor plan
remains very close to the original
house. Formal living and dining
rooms are warmed by wood-burning
fireplaces. Beyond, an expansive great
room is tucked away near the kitchen
and breakfast area. On the second
floor, a majestic three-storied tower
floods the second-floor hallway with
light. An additional stairway can be
constructed to the third floor and a
high-ceilinged tower room finished.
The four large bedrooms that occupy
the rest of the second floor include a
sumptuous master suite with elaborate closets and a compartmentalized
dressing area.

DESIGN	M8841
BEDROOMS	4
BATHROOMS	3½
FIRST FLOOR	1,582 Sq. Ft.
SECOND FLOOR	1,854 Sq. Ft.
TOTAL	3,436 Sq. Ft.
PRICE	C3

The first-floor guest bedroom in this charming residence lends great flexibility to the plan. If required, this room could function as a secluded study, hobby room, or a home office. An exceptionally generous breakfast bay provides ample room for family dining. The stairs rise conveniently from the great room, and lead to a spacious second-floor landing, well-lit by a Palladian window. The master suite houses a luxurious bath, with a corner tub and an angled shower. Both upstairs bedrooms feature oversized closets with ample room for clothes. Plans for detached garages for this home can be seen on pages 176 and 177.

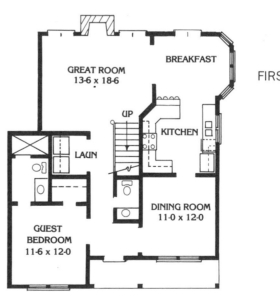

FIRST FLOOR

GREAT ROOM
13-6 x 18-6

BREAKFAST

UP

KITCHEN

LAUN

DINING ROOM
11-0 x 12-0

GUEST
BEDROOM
11-6 x 12-0

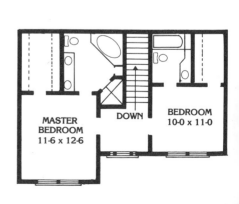

SECOND FLOOR

MASTER
BEDROOM
11-6 x 12-6

DOWN

BEDROOM
10-0 x 11-0

DESIGN	M8842
BEDROOMS	3
BATHROOMS	3½
FIRST FLOOR	1,093 Sq. Ft.
SECOND FLOOR	628 Sq. Ft.
TOTAL	1,721 Sq. Ft.
PRICE	C1

WIDTH 32'
DEPTH 39'

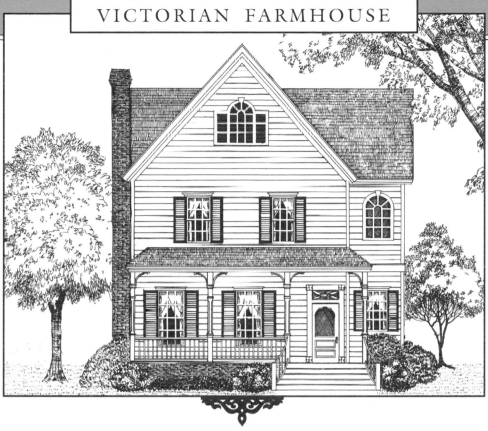

FIRST FLOOR

LAUNDRY BREAKFAST

KITCHEN

DINING ROOM
13-0 x 11-6

UP

GREAT ROOM
13-0 x 18-0

SECOND FLOOR

BEDROOM
11-6 x 14-0

BEDROOM
11-6 x 12-0

DOWN

MASTER
BEDROOM
14-0 x 14-0

WIDTH 32'
DEPTH 40'

The quaint and restful appeal of this peaceful Farmhouse design will make it suitable for either an urban or a rural setting. The openness of this plan lends the impression of a house much larger than its square footage reveals. The floor plan, with its careful attention to circulation, makes the house especially adaptable to entertaining. Ascending conveniently from the center of the house, the stairway is illuminated by two windows. The second-floor bedrooms are particularly spacious; the master includes two separate closets, as well as a compartmentalized bath and a whirlpool tub. Plans for detached garages for this home can be seen on pages 176 and 177.

DESIGN	M8843
BEDROOMS	3
BATHROOMS	2½
FIRST FLOOR	928 Sq. Ft.
SECOND FLOOR	875 Sq. Ft.
TOTAL	1,803 Sq. Ft.
PRICE	C1

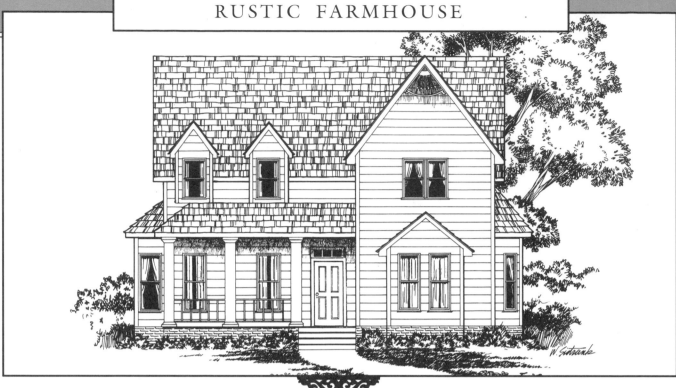

The 1868 edition of *Bicknell's Victorian Buildings* provided the inspiration for this classic home. The multiple bays that project from its clean and simple lines add architectural pizazz to the exterior and provide sunlit living spaces on the interior. An oversized dining room, ideal for displaying cherished antiques, opens off the foyer. Opposite this room, a commodious great room is warmed by a wood-burning fireplace. The first-floor guest suite can double as a secluded study. Upstairs, three oversized bedrooms possess an unusual amount of closet space; the master suite contains two separate closets. Plans for detached garages for this home can be seen on pages 176 and 177.

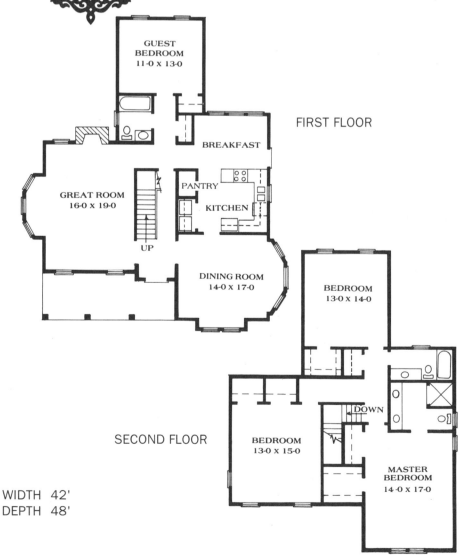

DESIGN	M8844
BEDROOMS	4
BATHROOMS	3
FIRST FLOOR	1,178 Sq. Ft.
SECOND FLOOR	1,078 Sq. Ft.
TOTAL	2,256 Sq. Ft.
PRICE	C2

WIDTH 42'
DEPTH 48'

FRENCH-TYPE FARMHOUSE

FIRST FLOOR

SECOND FLOOR

WIDTH 43'
DEPTH 45'

Board-and-batten siding, floor-to-ceiling windows, and a simplified porch railing contribute to the overall relaxed feeling of this French-style Farmhouse. Its familiar T-shape lends itself to natural ventilation and is a classic where seasons are moderate. Stairs that rise in the kitchen mean added convenience for a family on the go. The large walk-in closet provides ample storage for food supplies and serving pieces. An L-shaped rear porch is easily accessed from both the great room and the breakfast area. Above, a second-floor porch opens off the master suite and the back bedroom. Bedrooms feature a partitioned bath and walk-in closets. Plans for detached garages for this home can be seen on pages 176 and 177.

DESIGN	M8845
BEDROOMS	3
BATHROOMS	2½
FIRST FLOOR	1,190 Sq. Ft.
SECOND FLOOR	1,102 Sq. Ft.
TOTAL	2,292 Sq. Ft.
PRICE	C2

FOLK-TYPE FARMHOUSE

This Farmhouse design, with its long and welcoming porch, is a classic design that will never go out of style. An unusual floor plan, that isolates formal areas from family living, offers generously proportioned rooms perfect for displaying cherished antiques. The kitchen features a work island and a walk-in pantry for food storage; the butler's pantry that connects the kitchen and dining room is an ideal location for a wet bar. A rear staircase facilitates access to the bedrooms above. Here, three bedrooms are planned with a fourth room that can serve as a study or nursery. An unusually large amount of closet space is provided for those with storage needs. Plans for detached garages for this home can be found on pages 176 and 177.

FIRST FLOOR

LAUN
KITCHEN
BUTLER'S PANTRY
BREAKFAST
PAN
UP
DINING ROOM 12-6 x 14-0
GREAT ROOM 17-6 x 20-0
LIVING ROOM 12-6 x 12-6

SECOND FLOOR

BEDROOM 11-6 x 12-0
BEDROOM 11-6 x 12-0
DOWN
BATH
BATH
MASTER BEDROOM 14-0 x 16-6
STUDY 9-0 x 11-0

DESIGN	M8846
BEDROOMS	3
BATHROOMS	2½
FIRST FLOOR	1,332 Sq. Ft.
SECOND FLOOR	1,263 Sq. Ft.
TOTAL	2,595 Sq. Ft.
PRICE	C2

WIDTH 37'
DEPTH 48'

HISTORICAL REPLICATIONS, INC.

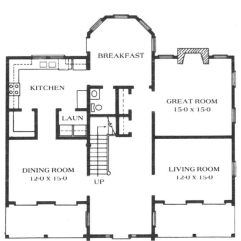

FIRST FLOOR

The front-facing gable that projects from the center of this inviting dwelling is highlighted by a glittering Palladian window. The magnificent foyer is open all the way to the ceiling of the second floor; this same Palladian contributes sunlight to both the first and second stories. In this very old-fashioned formal plan, a living room and dining room open onto separate front porches. Modern advancements, however, are apparent in the roomy country kitchen and bayed breakfast room. An oversized walk-in pantry is ample enough to contain a freezer, if desired. Above, the master suite reflects the bay below in a dazzling bathroom arrangement. Plans for detached garages for this home can be seen on pages 176 and 177.

SECOND FLOOR

WIDTH 44'
DEPTH 49'

DESIGN	M8847
BEDROOMS	4
BATHROOMS	2½
FIRST FLOOR	1,430 Sq. Ft.
SECOND FLOOR	1,160 Sq. Ft.
TOTAL	2,590 Sq. Ft.
PRICE	C2

CLASSIC FARMHOUSE

The front-facing gable of this classic Farmhouse accentuates the authentic transom-topped doorway below. The long front porch provides additional living space on temperate days. An exceptionally wide foyer instantly imparts an aura of spaciousness. The convenient walk-through bar connects the living room to the great room and facilitates entertaining. A spacious kitchen features a sizable walk-in pantry and a built-in desk. The handy laundry room has space for an upright freezer. Above, three bedrooms and the master suite are isolated from the noise of family living. The master bath, partitioned for comfort and privacy, has separate His and Hers closets. Plans for detached garages for this home can be seen on pages 176 and 177.

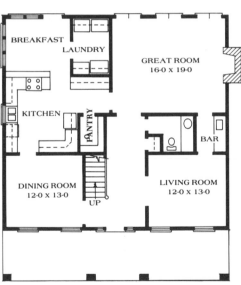

FIRST FLOOR

DESIGN	M8848
BEDROOMS	4
BATHROOMS	3½
FIRST FLOOR	1,368 Sq. Ft.
SECOND FLOOR	1,280 Sq. Ft.
TOTAL	2,648 Sq. Ft.
PRICE	C2

WIDTH 40'
DEPTH 36'

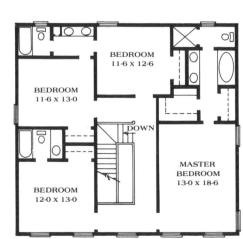

SECOND FLOOR

HISTORICAL REPLICATIONS, INC.

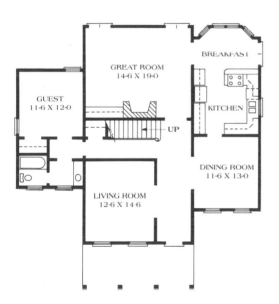

FIRST FLOOR

GUEST
11-6 X 12-0

GREAT ROOM
14-6 X 19-0

BREAKFAST

KITCHEN

UP

LIVING ROOM
12-6 X 14-6

DINING ROOM
11-6 X 13-0

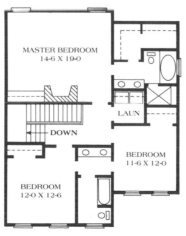

SECOND FLOOR

MASTER BEDROOM
14-6 X 19-0

DOWN

LAUN.

BEDROOM
11-6 X 12-0

BEDROOM
12-0 X 12-6

WIDTH 44'
DEPTH 48'

The irresistible appeal of this pleasing dwelling is due in part to its wide front porch. Additional enchantment emanates from the front-facing gable with its characteristic ornamentation. Inside, a centrally located stairway is an assist to family traffic patterns. The dining and kitchen wings open onto both formal and informal living areas to provide easy circulation. A private first-floor guest suite is isolated well away from other bedroom areas. Upstairs, the luxurious master suite has a wood-burning fireplace. The adjacent built-in can accommodate television or stereo equipment as well as books for bedtime reading. Two hall bedrooms share a compartmentalized bath. Plans for detached garages for this home can be seen on pages 176 and 177.

DESIGN	M8849
BEDROOMS	4
BATHROOMS	3
FIRST FLOOR	1,462 Sq. Ft.
SECOND FLOOR	1,112 Sq. Ft.
TOTAL	2,574 Sq. Ft.
PRICE	C2

The tantalizing porch of this classic Farmhouse design imparts charm and warmth to this impressive residence. An exceptionally wide entrance foyer, flanked by a living room and dining room, contributes to the aura of spaciousness and welcome. The roomy country kitchen with its long expanse of counter space is adjoined by a spacious utility room. Past the commodious great room, a secluded guest suite offers lucky visitors privacy and quiet. On the second floor, an expansive master suite contains two very large closets. Each of the hall bedrooms has its own private bath and walk-in closet. Plans for detached garages for this home can be seen on pages 176 and 177.

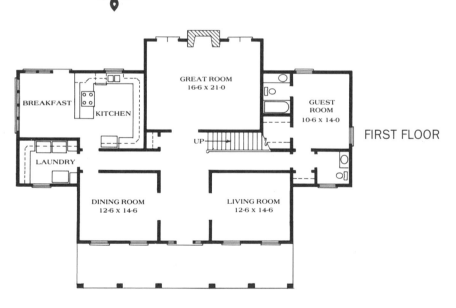

FIRST FLOOR

SECOND FLOOR

DESIGN   M8850
BEDROOMS   4
BATHROOMS   4½
FIRST FLOOR   1,884 Sq. Ft.
SECOND FLOOR   1,340 Sq. Ft.
TOTAL   3,224 Sq. Ft.
PRICE   C3

WIDTH 62'
DEPTH 46'

VICTORIAN FARMHOUSE

FIRST FLOOR

KITCHEN BREAKFAST
GREAT ROOM
17-6 x 20-6
LAUNDRY
LAU.
CHUTE
DINING ROOM
14-0 x 18-0
MASTER BEDROOM
16-6 x 18-6
LIVING ROOM
16-6 x 22-0
UP
STUDY
12-6 x 16-6

SECOND FLOOR

BEDROOM
14-0 x 14-0
DOWN
BEDROOM
12-0 x 16-6
BEDROOM
13-6 x 16-6
BEDROOM
12-0 x 16-6

WIDTH 60'
DEPTH 70'

The transom-topped entryway, crowned with a pedimented gable with graceful detailing, welcomes family and friends to this home. Within, a formal living and dining room, each with its own bay, reflect the original floor plan layout of this authentic replica. Across the wide hall, the master suite features a private study and sumptuous bath. The roomy country kitchen has a work island, a built-in desk, and adjoins an informal dining area and the great room. An old-fashioned butler's pantry connects the kitchen to the dining room. Above, four bedrooms share the two compartmentalized baths. Plans for detached garages for this home can be seen on pages 176 and 177.

DESIGN	M8851
BEDROOMS	5
BATHROOMS	3½
FIRST FLOOR	2,872 Sq. Ft.
SECOND FLOOR	1,600 Sq. Ft.
TOTAL	4,472 Sq. Ft.
PRICE	C4

This well-designed, detached garage plan beautifully complements any of the Victorian or Farmhouse designs shown on pages 124-175. Beneath its quaint hip roof is an area large enough for two cars. Attached is a giant area for garden tools, hobby or play equipment and other hard-to-store items. Choose the two-car option (M8852) or the three-car option (M8853).

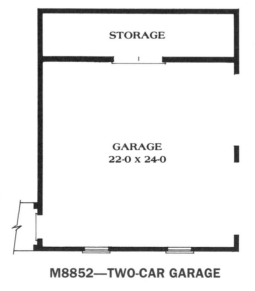

STORAGE

GARAGE
22-0 x 24-0

M8852—TWO-CAR GARAGE

DESIGN	M8852
SQUARE FOOTAGE	750
PRICE	C5

DESIGN	M8853
SQUARE FOOTAGE	782
PRICE	C6

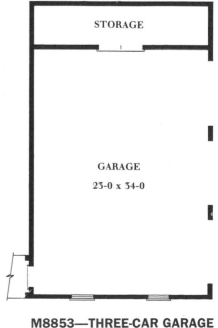

STORAGE

GARAGE
23-0 x 34-0

M8853—THREE-CAR GARAGE

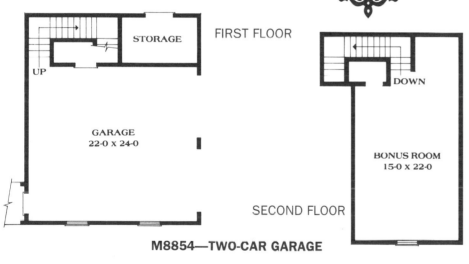

FIRST FLOOR

STORAGE

UP

GARAGE
22-0 x 24-0

DOWN

BONUS ROOM
15-0 x 22-0

SECOND FLOOR

M8854—TWO-CAR GARAGE

Here's an authentically styled, detached garage with an added attraction—a bonus room upstairs! This gable roofed plan fits well with any of the Victorian or Farmhouse designs shown on pages 124-175. Besides room for the family autos, there's storage space accessed from outside. Choose the two-car option (M8854) or the three-car option (M8855).

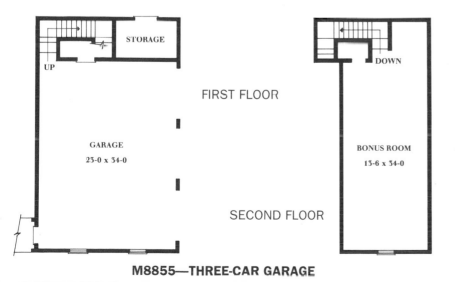

STORAGE

UP

FIRST FLOOR

GARAGE
23-0 x 34-0

DOWN

BONUS ROOM
13-6 x 34-0

SECOND FLOOR

M8855—THREE-CAR GARAGE

DESIGN	M8854
GARAGE	750 Sq. Ft.
BONUS ROOM	425 Sq. Ft.
TOTAL	1,175 Sq. Ft.
PRICE	C5

DESIGN	M8855
GARAGE	1,050 Sq. Ft.
BONUS ROOM	575 Sq. Ft.
TOTAL	1,625 Sq. Ft.
PRICE	C6

HISTORICAL REPLICATIONS, INC.

INCLUDED IN YOUR BLUEPRINTS ARE:

A Foundation Plan with a conventional crawl-space foundation layout including all necessary notations and dimensions. When an attached garage is part of the design, its concrete slab foundation and details are included also.

Fully Detailed Floor Plans reflecting all dimensions necessary for accurate framing and detailed layout and location of all electrical components and plumbing fixtures.

Exterior Elevations, which are views of the front, rear, right and left sides of your home. The finish materials and overall proportions and design are shown in these elevations.

Interior Elevations, which are interior views showing all kitchen, bath, fireplace, powder room, special built-ins and cabinet designs for your particular home.

A Complete Window And Door Schedule with sizes and styles recommended for the windows and doors included in the house design you select.

Building Cross Sections, cornice sections, fireplace sections and cabinet sections necessary to assist the builder in visualizing and understanding complicated interior details of major components of the home.

Framing Diagrams that show layouts of framing components and their locations for roof, first floor and second floor. This is especially important when a design consists of complex and unusual structural elements.

Energy Saving Details which specify such proven features as vapor barriers, insulated sheathing, caulking, foam sealant, batt insulation, wood windows and attic exhaust ventilators—in order to obtain R-19 in the walls and R-38 in the ceiling.

Typical Details And Sections displaying both interior and exterior techniques recommended in the completion of the design you have selected.

Note: All plans have been drawn to conform to basic FHA and VA regulations. Since the local codes for your area could vary slightly, modifications may be necessary to meet regional requirements.

Foundation Note: All of our plans are designed for a crawl-space foundation. Many of our designs can be readily adapted to a basement plan. An experienced builder can usually accomplish this alteration without our involvement; however, if interior or exterior design modifications are required, please contact a member of our staff for an estimate of our fee for this modification.

Some of our customers wish to build our houses on concrete slab foundations. In this situation, the interior floor plan must be slightly rearranged to allow for an HVAC closet and ductwork. Again, please call or write our offices for a quote on this type of alteration.

Mechanical Note: Heating and air conditioning layouts are not included in our plans. Your local mechanical contractor will size and locate the proper unit for your particular climatic conditions.

PRICE SCHEDULE

	C1	C2	C3	C4
One-set package	$350	$425	$500	$575
Five-set package	$420	$495	$550	$645
Eight-set package	$470	$545	$620	$695

Additional sets of working drawings $20
Mirror-reverse (dimensions & lettering will read backward) $25

	C5	C6
Garage Plans:	2-Car Garage	3-Car Garage
One-set package	$75	$90
Five-set package	$130	$145
Eight-set package	$170	$185

Additional sets of garage working drawings $15
Note: Additional sets can be ordered within 30 days of placing initial plan order.

TO ORDER BLUEPRINTS, TURN TO PAGE 187.

For more information on these plans, write:
Historical Replications, Inc., P.O. Box 13529, Jackson, Mississippi 39236

GREAT OUTDOOR PROJECTS

No house should go empty-landed for long. If you're searching for just the right structure to fill up those wide open spaces, we've got some solid choices to show you. Among these exciting plans you'll find a get-away-from-it-all gazebo that's big enough for small gatherings; a storage shed that does a number on clutter but looks great doing it; a two-dormer studio garage with all the comforts of home and a nice old-timey feel; and a gorgeous little crafts cottage with one very bright touch: an attached sunroom.

OUTDOOR PROJECTS INDEX & PRICE SCHEDULE

DESIGN		PAGE	PRICE	ADD'L SETS
MG106	Studio Garage	185	$75.00	$10.00
MG107	Storage Shed	184	$50.00	$10.00
MG108	Gazebo	180	$40.00	$10.00
MG109	Craft Cottage	181	$50.00	$10.00
MG110	Pool Cabana	182	$50.00	$10.00
MG292	Country Stable	183	$75.00	$10.00

TO ORDER, CALL TOLL FREE 1-800-521-6797, OR SEE PAGE 187.

Our gazebo is a prime spot for entertaining. At 200-plus square feet of decking, it has as much surface space as the average family room. Plus, it's just under 17½ feet tall, which makes it the size of a typical one-story house. As a result, it's best suited for larger lots—at least a half acre. Boasting a number of neo-classic features—perfect proportions, columns, bases—it's also a good match with Victorians and Farmhouses. The cupola is a homey touch that lets light in to the decking below. Cedar or redwood are the building materials of choice.

DESIGN MG108

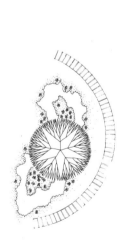

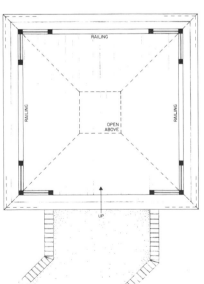

WIDTH 12'
DEPTH 12'

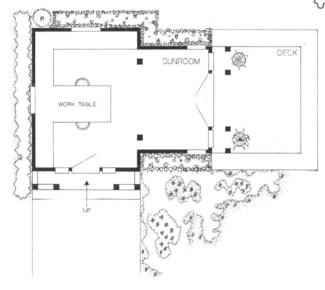

Great space for a cottage industry, this little building (250 square feet) is both functional and good looking. Ample counter space and shelving provide plenty of room to spread out materials and tools. Plus, a vaulted ceiling opens up the whole area. Next to the work space is a cozy sunroom (vaulted ceiling here, too). French doors and several windows, including a circle-head version above the doors, bathe the room in sunlight, while overhangs offer adequate shading. To get maximum sun, a south facing for the sunroom is best; it will also provide soft, even illumination for the north-facing work area.

DESIGN MG109

WIDTH 20'
DEPTH 16'

INTERIOR VIEW

Imagine this charming structure perched adjacent to your backyard swimming pool. Its exterior highlights such architectural features as hip and gable roofs, a decorative cupola, shuttered windows, flower boxes, and horizontal wood and shingle siding. Its plan offers a spacious sheltered party/lounge area with counter, sink and refrigerator space. An optional built-in table could assure no rain-outs of pool-side dining. Flanking this practical breezeway-type area are two rooms equal in size and utility. To the left is the changing room with a convenient bench. To the right is the equipment room for the handy storage of pool supplies and furniture. Surely a fine addition to the active family's backyard.

DESIGN MG110

WIDTH 24'
DEPTH 12' 8"

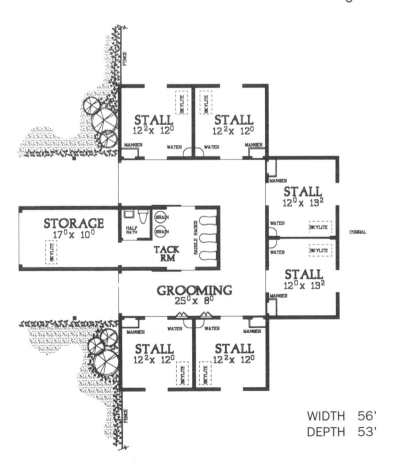

If you run a large operation, consider this expanded floor plan for your stable requirements. Six 12'-3" x 12' livestock pens with dirt floors feature built-in feed and water troughs and Dutch doors leading either to a fenced exercise area or into either of two conveniently located grooming areas. Both grooming areas have grooved cement floors, sloped for easy hosing and draining. A convenient connecting hall between the grooming areas also has sloped concrete floors for easy maintenance. A central secured tack room with built-in saddle racks and grain bins, a bath with a toilet and sink, and a 10' x 17' inside storage area for hay complete the available features. Nine skylights throughout the structure provide an abundance of natural light.

DESIGN MG292

WIDTH 56'
DEPTH 53'

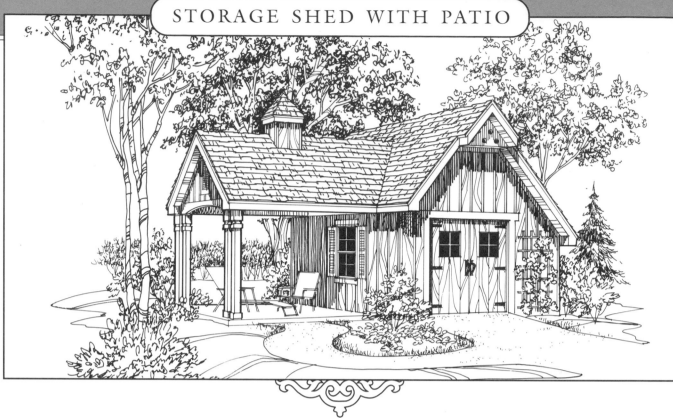

Here's a hard-working storage shed with a number of bright touches. At 120 square feet, it's bigger than most. Cupola, birdhouse, shutters, and grooved plywood siding add up to a traditional look that complements many popular housing styles—from Victorians to Farmhouses. It's a flexible design, too, and could also be a potting shed, lath-house or work-shop. The nicest feature may well be the covered patio. After you cut the grass, just stash the lawn mower, take a seat and survey your handiwork.

DESIGN MG107

WIDTH 12'
DEPTH 12'

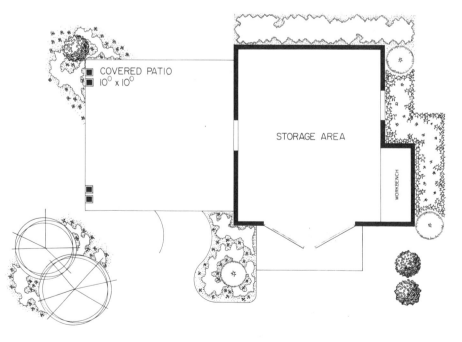

COVERED PATIO
10^0 x 10^0

STORAGE AREA

WORKBENCH

STUDIO
23⁴ x 13² +DORMERS

Can you top this? Our two-car garage has an artist's studio nestled snugly on the second floor. The Cape Cod-style design, with three dormers, large shutters, paneled doors and characteristic proportions of roof to floor, makes a strong visual statement that would complement a large number of traditional housing styles. An exterior staircase, covered at the top, leads to 445 square feet of fully insulated studio space, including a full 4x7-foot bath with shower and linen storage. The three-car design option (MG206) affords guest parking or extra storage space.

DESIGN MG106

GARAGE
23⁴ x 23⁴

WIDTH 24'
DEPTH 24'

LARRY W. GARNETT & ASSOCIATES

PLAN	SCHEDULE	PAGE
M8959	A3	63
M9000	A5	59
M9001	A4	57
M9002	A2	58
M9003	A4	56
M9004	A5	60
M9005	A5	61
M9006	A1	54
M9007	A1	53
M9008	A4	14
M9009	A4	20
M9010	A4	28
M9011	A4	29
M9012	A4	26
M9013	A5	41
M9014	A5	33
M9015	A5	47
M9016	A5	42
M9017	A5	39
M9030	A4	15
M9032	A1	48
M9033	A1	49
M9035	A1	50
M9038	A1	52
M9039	A1	51
M9049	A4	10
M9050	A1	12
M9051	A4	11
M9052	A4	13
M9053	A4	16
M9054	A1	17
M9055	A5	18
M9056	A4	19
M9057	A5	22
M9058	A4	23
M9059	A2	24
M9060	A2	25
M9061	A3	30
M9062	A5	31
M9063	A4	32
M9064	A3	34
M9065	A3	35
M9066	A4	36
M9067	A4	37
M9068	A2	38
M9069	A5	40
M9070	A6	43
M9071	A5	44
M9072	A3	45
M9073	A5	46
M9074	A1	55
M9075	A5	62

Price Schedules:

#Sets	A1	A2	A3	A4	A5/A6
One	$395	445	495	545	595
Four	445	495	545	595	645
Eight	490	540	590	640	695
Repro	590	640	690	740	795

Additional single sets	$40
Mirror Reverse Surcharge	$50
Materials List	$50

(not available on all plans, please inquire when ordering)

OUTDOOR PROJECTS

PLAN	PRICE	PAGE
MG106	$75	185
MG107	$50	184
MG108	$40	180
MG109	$50	181
MG110	$50	182
MG292	$75	183

HOME PLANNERS

PLAN	SCHEDULE	PAGE
M1956	B1	102
M2645	B3	85
M2646	B2	98
M2694	B3	106
M2774	B2	105
M2776	B2	110
M2829	B4	99
M2908	B2	103
M2946	B3	104
M2953	B5	95
M2954	B5	94
M2969	B3	84
M2970	B4	90
M2971	B3	82
M2973	B2	76
M2974	B1	67
M3304	B5	92
M3307	B3	81
M3308	B5	93
M3309	B2	77
M3382	B3	74
M3383	B3	66
M3384	B3	73
M3385	B3	68
M3386	B5	87
M3387	B5	89
M3388	B4	79
M3389	B3	70
M3390	B3	69
M3392	B4	88
M3393	B3	72
M3394	B4	78
M3395	B5	86
M3396	B3	112
M3397	B4	114
M3398	B3	115
M3399	B4	113
M3438	B3	117
M3466	B2	119
M3468	B2	118
M3469	B2	116
M3512	B4	71
M3522	B2	80
M3619	B2	111
M3620	B2	96
M3621	B3	97
M3653	B3	108
M3673	B1	100
M3674	B2	107
M3677	B2	120
M3678	B2	101
M3681	B2	109
M3696	B2	121

Price Schedules:

	B1	B2	B3	B4	B5
1-set Study Pkg.	$350	$390	$430	$470	$590
4-set Building Pkg.	$395	$435	$475	$515	$635
8-set Building Pkg.	$455	$495	$535	$575	$695
1-set Reproducible Sepias	$555	$615	$675	$735	$795
Home Customizer® Pkg.	$605	$665	$725	$785	$845

Additional Identical Blueprints in same order	$50 per set
Reverse Blueprints (Mirror Image)	$50 per set
Specification Outlines	$10 each
Materials List	
Schedule B1-B4	$50 each
Schedule B5	$60 each
Additional Materials Lists in same order	$10 each

HISTORICAL REPLICATIONS

PLAN	SCHEDULE	PAGE
M8800	C1	124
M8801	C1	125
M8802	C1	126
M8803	C1	130
M8804	C1	128
M8805	C2	138
M8806	C1	127
M8807	C1	143
M8808	C1	132
M8809	C1	133
M8810	C1	131
M8811	C1	129
M8812	C2	134
M8813	C2	135
M8814	C1	136
M8815	C2	137
M8816	C2	140
M8817	C1	141
M8818	C2	144
M8819	C2	145
M8820	C2	139
M8821	C2	148
M8822	C2	146
M8823	C2	142
M8824	C2	150
M8825	C2	151
M8826	C2	147
M8827	C2	149
M8828	C2	152
M8829	C2	153
M8830	C2	154
M8831	C2	155
M8832	C2	156
M8833	C2	157
M8834	C2	158
M8835	C2	159
M8836	C2	160
M8837	C2	161
M8838	C3	162
M8839	C2	163
M8840	C3	164
M8841	C3	165
M8842	C1	166
M8843	C1	167
M8844	C2	168
M8845	C2	169
M8846	C2	170
M8847	C2	171
M8848	C2	172
M8849	C2	173
M8850	C3	174
M8851	C4	175
M8852	C5	176
M8853	C6	176
M8854	C5	177
M8855	C6	177

Price Schedules:

	C1	C2	C3	C4
One-set pkg.	$350	$425	$500	$575
Five-set pkg.	$420	$495	$550	$645
Eight-set pkg.	$470	$545	$620	$695

Additional sets of working drawings	$20
Mirror Reverse (dimensions and lettering will read backward)	$25

	C5	C6
Garage Plans:	2-Car Garage	3-Car Garage
One-set pkg.	$75	$90
Five-set pkg.	$130	$145
Eight-set pkg.	$170	$185

Additional sets of garage working drawings ... $15

Note: Additional sets can be ordered within 30 days of placing initial plan order.

Before You Order . . .

Before filling out the coupon at right or calling us on our Toll-Free Blueprint Hotline, you may want to learn more about our services and products. Here's some information you will find helpful.

Quick Turnaround
We process and ship every blueprint order from our office within 48 hours. Because of this quick turnaround, we won't send a formal notice acknowledging receipt of your order.

Our Exchange Policy
Since blueprints are printed in response to your order, we cannot honor requests for refunds. However, we will exchange your entire first order for an equal number of blueprints at a price of $50 for the first set and $10 for each additional set; $70 total exchange fee for 4 sets; $100 total exchange fee for 8 sets . . . plus the difference in cost if exchanging for a design in a higher price bracket or less the difference in cost if exchanging for a design in lower price bracket. One exchange is allowed within a year of purchase date. (Sepias are not exchangeable.) All sets from the first order must be returned before the exchange can take place. Please add $10 for postage and handling via ground service; $20 via Second Day Air; $30 via Next Day Air.

About Reverse Blueprints
If you want to build in reverse of the plan as shown, we will include an extra set of reverse blueprints (mirror image) for an additional fee of $50. Although lettering and dimensions will appear backward, reverses will be a useful aid if you decide to flop the plan.

Revising, Modifying and Customizing Plans
The wide variety of designs available in this publication allows you to select ideas and concepts for a home to fit your building site and match your family's needs, wants and budget. Like many homeowners who buy these plans, you and your builder, architect or engineer may want to make changes to them. Some minor changes may be made by your builder, but we recommend that most changes be made by a licensed architect or engineer. If you need to make alterations to a design that is customizable, you need only order our Home Customizer® Package to get you started. As set forth below, we cannot assume any responsibility for blueprints which have been changed, whether by you, your builder or by professionals selected by you or referred to you by us, because such individuals are outside our supervision and control.

Architectural and Engineering Seals
Some cities and states are now requiring that a licensed architect or engineer review and "seal" a blueprint, or officially approve it, prior to construction due to concerns over energy costs, safety and other factors. Prior to application for a building permit or the start of actual construction, we strongly advise that you consult your local building official who can tell you if such a review is required.

About the Designers
The architects and designers whose work appears in this publication are among America's leading residential designers. Each plan was designed to meet the requirements of a nationally recognized model building code in effect at the time and place the plan was drawn. Because national building codes change from time to time, plans may not comply with any such code at the time they are sold to a customer. In addition, building officials may not accept these plans as final construction documents of record as the plans may need to be modified and additional drawings and details added to suit local conditions and requirements. We strongly advise that purchasers consult a licensed architect or engineer, and their local building official, before starting any construction related to these plans.

Local Building Codes and Zoning Requirements
At the time of creation, our plans are drawn to specifications published by the Building Officials and Code Administrators (BOCA) International, Inc.; the Southern Building Code Congress (SBCCI) International, Inc.; the International Conference of Building Officials; or the Council of American Building Officials (CABO). Our plans are designed to meet or exceed national building standards. Because of the great differences in geography and climate throughout the United States and Canada, each state, county and municipality has its own building codes, zone requirements, ordinances and building regulations. Your plan may need to be modified to comply with local requirements regarding snow loads, energy codes, soil and seismic conditions and a wide range of other matters. In addition, you may need to obtain permits or inspections from local governments before and in the course of construction. Prior to using blueprints ordered from us, we strongly advise that you consult a licensed architect or engineer—and speak with your local building official—before applying for any permit or beginning construction. We authorize the use of our blueprints on the express condition that you strictly comply with all local building codes, zoning requirements and other applicable laws, regulations, ordinances and requirements.

Notice: Plans for homes to be built in Nevada must be re-drawn by a Nevada-registered professional. Consult your building official for more information on this subject.

Foundation and Exterior Wall Changes
Most of our plans are drawn with either a full or partial basement foundation. Depending on your specific climate or regional building practices, you may wish to change this basement to a slab or crawl-space. Most professional contractors and builders can easily adapt your plans to alternate foundation types. Likewise, most can easily change 2x4 wall construction to 2x6, or vice versa.

Disclaimer
We and the designers we work with have put substantial care and effort into the creation of our blueprints. However, because we cannot provide on-site consultation, supervision and control over actual construction, and because of the great variance in local building requirements, building practices and soil, seismic, weather and other conditions, WE CANNOT MAKE ANY WARRANTY, EXPRESS OR IMPLIED, WITH RESPECT TO THE CONTENT OR USE OF OUR BLUEPRINTS, INCLUDING BUT NOT LIMITED TO ANY WARRANTY OF MERCHANTABILITY OR OF FITNESS FOR A PARTICULAR PURPOSE.

Terms and Conditions
The terms and conditions governing our license of blueprints to you are set forth in the material accompanying the blueprints. This material tells you how to return the blueprints if you do not agree to these terms and conditions.

Canadian Customers
Order Toll-Free 1-800-561-4169

For faster service and plans that are modified for building in Canada, customers may now call in orders directly to our Canadian supplier of plans and charge the purchase to a charge card. Or, you may complete the order form at right, adding 40% to all prices and mail in Canadian funds to:

The Plan Centre 60 Baffin Place, Unit 5
Waterloo, Ontario N2V 1Z7

OR: Copy the order form and send it via our Canadian FAX line: 1-800-719-3291.

HOME PLANNERS
A DIVISION OF HANLEY-WOOD, INC.
3275 W. INA ROAD, SUITE 110
TUCSON, AZ 85741

BASIC BLUEPRINT PACKAGE—ALL DESIGNERS
Rush me the following (please refer to the Plan and Price Index opposite):

____ Set(s) of blueprints for plan number _____ $ _____
____ Set(s) of reproducible sepias for plan number _____ $ _____
____ Set(s) of additional identical blueprints in same order $ _____
____ Set(s) of reverse blueprints $ _____
____ Set(s) of Historical Replications garage plan number _____ $ _____

EXTRAS FOR HOME PLANNERS' PLANS ONLY
____ Materials Lists @ $50.00 first set Schedule B1-B4; $60.00 first set Schedule B5: Additional sets $10.00 each $ _____
____ Quote One® Summary Cost Report @ $19.95 each, $14.95 for each additional, for plans _____ $ _____
Building Location: City _____ Zip Code _____
____ Quote One® Materials Cost Report @ $110 Schedules B1-B4 or $120 for Schedule B5, for plan _____ $ _____
(Must be purchased with blueprints set)
Building Location: City _____ Zip Code _____

IMPORTANT EXTRAS FOR USE WITH ANY PLAN
(see Extra Products section, pages 188-189, for details)
____ Specification Outlines @ $10.00 each _____ $ _____
____ Detail Sets @ $14.95 each; any two for $22.95; all three for $29.95; all four for $39.95 (save $19.85) $ _____
____Plumbing ____Electrical ____Construction ____Mechanical
(These helpful details provide general construction advice and are not too specific to any single plan.)
____ Plan-A-Home® @ $29.95 each $ _____
____ Set(s) of blueprints for Outdoor Project number(s) _____ $ _____

POSTAGE AND HANDLING	1-3 sets	4 or more sets	
DELIVERY (Requires street address—No P.O. Boxes)			
• Regular Service Allow 4-6 days delivery	$15.00	$18.00	$_____
• Priority Allow 2-3 days delivery	$20.00	$30.00	$_____
• Express Allow 1 day delivery	$30.00	$40.00	$_____
CERTIFIED MAIL (Requires signature) Allow 4-6 days delivery	$20.00	$30.00	$_____

OVERSEAS DELIVERY Fax, phone or mail for quote.
Note: All delivery times are from date of shipment.

POSTAGE $ _____
SUBTOTAL $ _____
SALES TAX: (AZ, CA, NY, DC, IL, MI, MN, and WA residents please add appropriate state and local sales tax.) $ _____
TOTAL (Sub-total and tax) $ _____

YOUR ADDRESS (Please Print):

Name _____
Street _____
City _____ State _____ Zip _____
Daytime telephone number _____

FOR CREDIT CARD ORDERS ONLY ☐ MasterCard
Please fill in the information below ☐ Visa ☐ Discover

Credit Card Number _____ Exp. Month/Year _____ / _____

Signature _____ Order Form Key TB21

Introducing eight important planning and construction aids developed by our professionals to help you succeed in your home-building project.

MATERIALS LIST

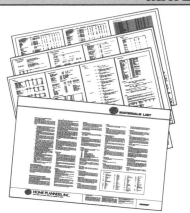

For many of the designs in our portfolio, we offer a customized materials take-off that is invaluable in planning and estimating the cost of your new home. This Materials List outlines the quantity, type and size of materials needed to build your house (with the exception of mechanical system items). Included are framing lumber, windows and doors, kitchen and bath cabinetry, rough and finish hardware, and much more. This handy list helps you or your builder cost out materials and serves as a reference sheet when you're compiling bids.

(Note: Because of the diversity of local building codes, our Materials List does not include mechanical materials.)

SPECIFICATION OUTLINE

This valuable 16-page document is critical to building your house correctly. Designed to be filled in by you or your builder, this book lists 166 stages or items crucial to the building process. It provides a comprehensive review of the construction process and helps in making choices of materials. When combined with the blueprints, a signed contract, and a schedule, it becomes a legal document and record for the building of your home.

QUOTE ONE®

Summary Cost Report / Materials Cost Report

A new service for estimating the cost of building select designs, the Quote One® system is available in two separate stages: The Summary Cost Report and the Materials Cost Report.

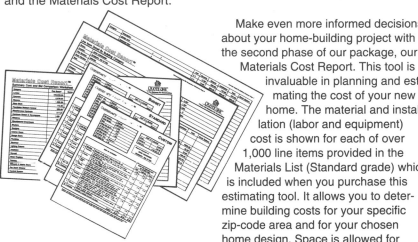

Make even more informed decisions about your home-building project with the second phase of our package, our Materials Cost Report. This tool is invaluable in planning and estimating the cost of your new home. The material and installation (labor and equipment) cost is shown for each of over 1,000 line items provided in the Materials List (Standard grade) which is included when you purchase this estimating tool. It allows you to determine building costs for your specific zip-code area and for your chosen home design. Space is allowed for additional estimates from contractors and subcontractors, such as for mechanical materials, which are not included in our packages. This invaluable tool is available for a price of $110 ($120 for a Schedule E plan) which includes a Materials List.

The Summary Cost Report is the first stage in the package and shows the total cost per square foot for your chosen home in your zip-code area and then breaks that cost down into ten categories showing the costs for building materials, labor and installation. The total cost for the report (which includes three grades: Budget, Standard and Custom) is just $19.95 for one home, and additionals are only $14.95. These reports allow you to evaluate your building budget and compare the costs of building a variety of homes in your area.

To order these invaluable reports, use the order form on page 187 or call 1-800-521-6797.

DETAIL SHEETS

If you want to know more about techniques—and deal more confidently with subcontractors—we offer these remarkably useful detail sheets. Each is an excellent tool that will enhance your understanding of these technical subjects.

Plan-A-Home®

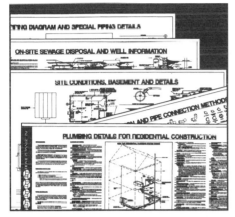

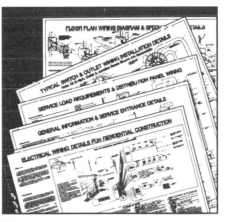

PLUMBING

The Blueprint Package includes locations for all the plumbing fixtures in your new house. However, if you want to know more about the complete plumbing system, these 24x36-inch detail sheets will prove very useful. Prepared to meet requirements of the National Plumbing Code, these six fact-filled sheets give general information on pipe schedules, fittings, sump-pump details, water-softener hookups, septic system details and much more.

ELECTRICAL

The locations for every electrical switch, plug and outlet are shown in your Blueprint Package. However, these Electrical Details go further to take the mystery out of household electrical systems. Prepared to meet requirements of the National Electrical Code, these comprehensive 24x36-inch drawings come packed with helpful information, including wire sizing, switch-installation schematics, cable-routing details, appliance wattage, door-bell hook-ups, typical service panel circuitry and much more.

Plan-A-Home® is an easy-to-use tool that helps you design a new home, arrange furniture in a new or existing home, or plan a remodeling project. Each package contains:

• **More than 700 reusable peel-off planning symbols** on a self-stick vinyl sheet, including walls, windows, doors, all types of furniture, kitchen components, bath fixtures and many more.

• **A reusable, transparent, 1/4-inch scale planning grid** that matches the scale of actual working drawings (1/4-inch equals 1 foot). This grid provides the basis for house layouts of up to 140x92 feet.

• **Tracing paper** and a protective sheet for copying or transferring your completed plan.

• **A felt-tip pen,** with water-soluble ink that wipes away quickly.

Plan-A-Home® lets you lay out areas as large as a 7,500 square foot, six-bedroom, seven-bath house.

CONSTRUCTION

The Blueprint Package contains everything an experienced builder needs to construct a particular house. However, it doesn't show all the ways that houses can be built, nor does it explain alternate construction methods. To help you understand how your house will be built—and offer additional techniques—this set of drawings depicts the materials and methods used to build foundations, fireplaces, walls, floors and roofs. These six sheets will answer questions for the advanced do-it-yourselfer or home planner.

MECHANICAL

This package contains fundamental principles and useful data that will help you make informed decisions and communicate with subcontractors about heating and cooling systems. The 24x36-inch drawings contain instructions and samples that allow you to make simple load calculations and preliminary sizing and costing analysis. Covered are today's most commonly used systems from heat pumps to solar fuel systems.

To Order, Call Toll Free 1-800-521-6797

To add these important extras to your Blueprint Package, simply indicate your choices on the order form on page 187 or call us Toll Free 1-800-521-6797 and we'll tell you more about these exciting products.

Home Planners wants your building experience to be as pleasant and trouble-free as possible. That's why we've expanded our library of Do-It-Yourself titles to help you along. In addition to our beautiful plans books, we've added books to guide you through specific projects as well as the construction process. In fact, these are titles that will be as useful after your dream home is built as they are right now.

ONE-STORY

1 448 designs for all lifestyles. 860 to 5,400 square feet. 384 pages $9.95

TWO-STORY

2 460 designs for one-and-a-half and two stories. 1,245 to 7,275 square feet. 384 pages $9.95

VACATION

3 345 designs for recreation, retirement and leisure. 312 pages $8.95

MULTI-LEVEL
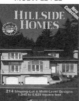
4 312 designs for split-levels, bi-levels, multi-levels and walkouts. 224 pages $8.95

COUNTRY

5 200 country designs from classic to contemporary by 7 winning designers. 224 pages $8.95

MOVE-UP

6 200 stylish designs for today's growing families from 9 hot designers. 224 pages $8.95

NARROW-LOT

7 200 unique homes less than 60' wide from 7 designers. Up to 3,000 square feet. 224 pages $8.95

SMALL HOUSE

8 200 beautiful designs chosen for versatility and affordability. 224 pages $8.95

BUDGET-SMART

9 200 efficient plans from 7 top designers, that you can really afford to build! 224 pages $8.95

EXPANDABLES

10 200 flexible plans that expand with your needs from 7 top designers. 240 pages $8.95

ENCYCLOPEDIA

11 500 exceptional plans for all styles and budgets—the best book of its kind! 352 pages $9.95

AFFORDABLE

12 Completely revised and updated, featuring 300 designs for modest budgets. 256 pages $9.95

ENCYCLOPEDIA 2

13 500 Completely new plans. Spacious and stylish designs for every budget and taste. 352 pages $9.95

VICTORIAN

14 160 striking Victorian and Farmhouse designs from three leading designers. 192 pages $12.95

EASY-LIVING

15 216 Efficient and sophisticated plans that are small in size, but big on livability. 224 pages $8.95

LUXURY

16 154 fine luxury plans-loaded with luscious amenities! 192 pages $14.95

LIGHT-FILLED

17 223 great designs that make the most of natural sunlight. 240 pages $8.95

BEST SELLERS

18 Our 50th Anniversary book with 200 of our very best designs in full color! 224 pages $12.95

SPECIAL COLLECTION

19 70 Romantic house plans that capture the classic tradition of home design. 160 pages $17.95

COUNTRY HOUSES

20 208 Unique home plans that combine traditional style and modern livability. 224 pages $9.95

TRADITIONAL

21 403 designs of classic beauty and elegance. 304 pages $9.95

MODERN & CLASSIC

22 341 impressive homes featuring the latest in contemporary design. 304 pages $9.95

NEW ENGLAND

23 260 of the best in Colonial home design. Special interior design sections, too. 384 pages $14.95

SOUTHERN

24 207 homes rich in Southern styling and comfort. 240 pages $8.95

Landscape Designs

Outdoor Projects

SUNBELT

25 215 Designs that capture the spirit of the Southwest. 208 pages $10.95

WESTERN

26 215 designs that capture the spirit and diversity of the Western lifestyle. 208 pages $9.95

EASY CARE

27 41 special landscapes designed for beauty and low maintenance. 160 pages $14.95

FRONT & BACK

28 The first book of do-it-yourself landscapes. 40 front, 15 backyards. 208 pages $14.95

BACKYARDS

29 40 designs focused solely on creating your own specially themed backyard oasis. 160 pages $14.95

OUTDOOR

30 42 unique outdoor projects. Gazebos, strombellas, bridges, sheds, playsets and more! 96 pages $7.95

GARAGES & MORE

31 101 Multi-use garages and outdoor structures to enhance any home. 96 pages $7.95

DECKS

32 25 outstanding single-, double- and multi-level decks you can build. 112 pages $7.95

Design Software

BOOK & CD ROM	3D DESIGN SUITE	ENERGY GUIDE	BATHROOMS	KITCHENS	HOUSE CONTRACTING	WINDOWS & DOORS	CONTRACTING GUIDE

33 Both the Home Planners Gold book and matching Windows™ CD ROM with 3D floorplans. $24.95

34 Home design made easy! View designs in 3D, take a virtual reality tour, add decorating details and more. $59.95

35 The most comprehensive energy efficiency and conservation guide available. 280 pages $35.00

36 An innovative guide to organizing, remodeling and decorating your bathroom. 96 pages $8.95

37 An imaginative guide to designing the perfect kitchen. Chock full of bright ideas to make your job easier. 176 pages $14.95

38 Everything you need to know to act as your own general contractor...and save up to 25% off building costs. 134 pages $12.95

39 Installation techniques and tips that make your project easier and more professional looking. 80 pages $7.95

40 Loaded with information to make you more confident in dealing with contractors and subcontractors. 287 pages $18.95

ROOFING	FRAMING	VISUAL HANDBOOK	BASIC WIRING	PATIOS & WALKS	TILE	PLUMBING	TRIM & MOLDING

41 Information on the latest tools, materials and techniques for roof installation or repair. 80 pages $7.95

42 For those who want to take a more-hands on approach to their dream. 319 pages $19.95

43 A plain-talk guide to the construction process; financing to final walk-through, this book covers it all. 498 pages $19.95

44 A straight forward guide to one of the most misunderstood systems in the home. 160 pages $12.95

45 Clear step-by-step instructions take you from the basic design stages to the finished project. 80 pages $7.95

46 Every kind of tile for every kind of application. Includes tips on use installation and repair. 176 pages $12.95

47 Tackle any plumbing installation or repair as quickly and efficiently as a professional. 160 pages $12.95

48 Step-by-step instructions for installing baseboards, window and door casings and more. 80 pages $7.95

Additional Books Order Form

To order your books, just check the box of the book numbered below and complete the coupon. We will process your order and ship it from our office within 48 hours. Send coupon and check (in U.S. funds).

YES! Please send me the books I've indicated:

☐ 1:VO $9.95	☐ 25:SW $10.95
☐ 2:VT $9.95	☐ 26:WH $9.95
☐ 3:VH $8.95	☐ 27:ECL $14.95
☐ 4:VS $8.95	☐ 28:HL $14.95
☐ 5:FH $8.95	☐ 29:BYL $14.95
☐ 6:MU $8.95	☐ 30:YG $7.95
☐ 7:NL $8.95	☐ 31:GG $7.95
☐ 8:SM $8.95	☐ 32:DP $7.95
☐ 9:BS $8.95	☐ 33:HPGC $24.95
☐ 10:EX $8.95	☐ 34:PLANSUITE . . $59.95
☐ 11:EN $9.95	☐ 35:RES $35.00
☐ 12:AF $9.95	☐ 36:CDP $9.95
☐ 13:E2 . . . . $9.95	☐ 37:CDB $8.95
☐ 14:VDH $12.95	☐ 38:CKI $14.95
☐ 15:EL $8.95	☐ 39:SBC $12.95
☐ 16:LD2 . . . . $14.95	☐ 40:BCC $18.95
☐ 17:NA $8.95	☐ 41:CGR $7.95
☐ 18:HPG $12.95	☐ 42:SRF $19.95
☐ 19:WEP $17.95	☐ 43:RVH $19.95
☐ 20:CN $9.95	☐ 44:CBW $12.95
☐ 21:ET $9.95	☐ 45:CGW $7.95
☐ 22:EC $9.95	☐ 46:CWT $12.95
☐ 23:NES $14.95	☐ 47:CMP $12.95
☐ 24:SH $8.95	☐ 48:CGT $7.95

Canadian Customers
Order Toll-Free 1-800-561-4169

Additional Books Sub-Total $ _____
ADD Postage and Handling $ __3.00__
Sales Tax: (AZ, CA, NY, DC, IL, MI, MN, and WA residents please add appropriate state and local sales tax.) $ _____
YOUR TOTAL (Sub-Total, Postage/Handling, Tax) $ _____

YOUR ADDRESS (Please print)

Name _____

Street _____

City _____ State _____ Zip _____

Phone (_____) _____ — _____

YOUR PAYMENT
Check one: ☐ Check ☐ Visa ☐ MasterCard ☐ Discover Card
Required credit card information:

Credit Card Number _____

Expiration Date (Month/Year) _____ / _____

Signature Required _____

 Home Planners, A Division of Hanley-Wood, Inc.
3275 W Ina Road, Suite 110, Dept. BK, Tucson, AZ 85741

TB21

Architectural Antiques Exchange
715 N. Second St.
Philadelphia, PA 19123
(215) 922-3669
Fax (215) 922-3680
doors, entryways, fencing & gates, windows, mantels, bars, backbars, vintage plumbing

Anthony Wood Products, Inc.
P.O. Box 1081
Hillsboro, TX 76645
(817) 582-7225
FAX (817) 582-7620
arches, balusters, brackets, corbels, drops, finials, fretwork, gable trim, spindles, exterior porch parts

The Balmer Architectural Art Studios
9 Codeco Court
Don Mills, ONT M3A 1B6 Canada
(416) 449-2155
FAX (416) 449-3018
cartouches, centerpieces, festoons, finials, friezes, keystones, medallions, mouldings, pilasters, rosettes

Blue Ox Millworks
Foot of X St.
Eureka, CA 95501-0847
(800) 248-4259 (707) 444-3437
FAX (707) 444-0918
balusters, baseboards, doors & windows, gutters, mouldings, porches, posts, vergeboards, wainscoting

Cain Architectural Art Glass
Rt. 1 Box AAA
Bremo Bluff, VA 23022
(804) 842-3984
FAX (804) 842-1021
beveled glass, windows, custom beveling on traditional machinery

Classic Architectural Specialties
3223 Canton St.
Dallas, TX 75226
(214) 748-1668 (in Dallas)
(800) 662-1221
FAX (214) 748-7149
uncommon architectural features

Creative Openings
P.O. Box 4204
Bellingham, WA 98227
(360) 671-6420
FAX (360) 671-0207
screen doors

Cumberland Woodcraft Co.
P.O. Drawer 609
Carlisle, PA 17013
(800) 367-1884 (outside of PA)
(717) 243-0063
FAX (717) 243-6502
balusters, brackets, carvings, corbels, doors, fretwork, mouldings, screen doors

Custom Ironwork, Inc.
P.O. Box 180
Union, KY 41091
(606) 384-4122
FAX (606) 384-4848
fencing & gates

Denninger Cupolas & Weathervanes
RD 1, Box 447
Middletown, NY 10940
(914) 343-2229 (Phone and Fax)
Internet site: www.denninger.com
cupolas, weather vanes, finials, caps

Elegant Entries
240 Washington St.
Auburn, MA 01501
(800) 343-3432
(508) 832-9898 (in MA)
FAX (508) 832-6874
beveled glass, doors, art glass

Focal Point Inc.
P.O. Box 93327
Atlanta, GA 30377-0327
(800) 662-5550 (404) 351-0820
FAX (404) 352-9049
arches, centerpieces, door & window casings, entryways, festoons, friezes, keystones, medallions, mouldings, rosettes

Gothom, Inc.
Box 421, 110 Main St.
Erin, ONT N0B 1T0 Canada
(519) 371-8345
FAX (519) 371-8268
balusters, porches, posts, screen doors, vergeboards

Mad River Woodworks Co.
Box 1067
Blue Lake, CA 95525-1067
(707) 668-5671
FAX (707) 668-5673
brackets, drops, entryways, finials, mouldings, posts, spandrels, wainscoting, siding, shingles

W.F. Norman Corporation
P.O. Box 323, 214 N. Cedar
Nevada, MO 64772-0323
(800) 641-4038 (417) 667-5552
FAX (417) 667-2708
balusters, brackets, cartouches, finials, friezes, keystones, mouldings, tin ceilings, metal roofs, siding

The Old Wagon Factory
P.O. Box 1427, Dept. PHE91
Clarksville, VA 23927
(804) 374-5787
FAX (804) 374-4646
storm screens

Ornamental Mouldings Limited
P.O. Box 336
Waterloo, ONT N2J 4A4 Canada
(519) 884-4080
FAX (519) 884-9692
in the United States:
P.O. Box 4068
Archdale, NC 27263-4068
baseboards, door & window casings, mouldings

The Renovators Supply
P.O. Box 2515
Conway, NH 03818
(800) 659-2211
FAX (603) 447-1717
classic hardware, plumbing, lighting and home decorating items

San Francisco Victoriana, Inc.
2070 Newcomb Ave.
San Francisco, CA 94124
(415) 648-0313
FAX (415) 648-2812
baseboards, brackets, centerpieces, door and window casings, festoons, medallions, mouldings, pilasters, posts, rosettes, wainscoting

The Millworks Inc.
P.O. Box 2987 - HPI
Durango, CO 81302
(800) 933-3930 (970) 259-5915
FAX (970) 259-5919
arches, balusters, baseboards, brackets, carvings, door and window casings, drops, keystones, mouldings, pilasters, porches, posts, screen doors, vergeboards, wainscoting, windows

Tennessee Fabricating Co.
2025 York Ave.
Memphis, TN 38104
(901) 725-1548
FAX (901) 725-5954
brackets, fencing & gates, finials, porches

Vintage Wood Works
Highway 34
P.O. Box R
Quinlan, TX 75474
(903) 356-2158
FAX (903) 356-3023
arches, balusters, brackets, corbels, drops, finials, fretwork, gable decorations, porches, posts, spandrels, vergeboards